ECOLOGY CONTESTED

ECOLOGY CONTESTED

Environmental Politics between Left and Right

Peter Staudenmaier

lode.press

Ecology Contested: Environmental Politics between Left and Right
2021 © by Peter Staudenmaier

ISBN 978-82-93064-57-2
ISBN 978-82-93064-58-9 (ebook)

Published by New Compass Press
Porsgrunn, Norway

Design and layout by Eirik Eiglad

New Compass presents ideas on participatory democracy, social ecology,
and movement building—for a free, secular, and ecological society.

lode.press
2021

Contents

Preface

The essays collected in this volume were written between 1998 and 2020. Earlier versions of several of them have appeared previously: "Disney Ecology" was originally published in 1998 as a pamphlet for the Institute for Social Ecology, and subsequently re-published in the Summer 2001 issue of the anarchist periodical *Onward*; "Ambiguities of Animal Rights" was originally published in *Communalism* no. 5 in 2003; "The Politics of Nature" was originally published in the Fall 2020 issue of the Institute for Social Ecology's online journal *Harbinger*. The remaining essays appear here for the first time.

Much of the material explored in this book developed from my involvement in various radical environmental movements in the United States and Germany. The activists I met in the 1980s and 1990s in groups like the Left Green

Network and the *Ökologische Linke*, as well as the faculty and students at the Institute for Social Ecology, consistently challenged and sharpened my viewpoint on these issues. In those contexts and others, I have been a vocal critic of some of the more regressive strands within the environmental milieu. This longstanding engagement with the contentious politics of ecology has shaped my perceptions of the past just as it has shaped my perspective on the present.

I am indebted to many people who have helped form the ideas and arguments I present in this book. For reading early drafts and offering critical comments, I would like to thank Eirik Eiglad, Eleanor Finley, Chaia Heller, Emma Kuby, Mike Staudenmaier, and Spencer Sunshine. For spirited debates, help with sources, and general support I thank Christine Achinger, Hamish Alcorn, Ashanti Alston, Sina Arnold, Gizem Arslan, Kazembe Balagun, Mark Bassin, Chip Berlet, Janet Biehl, Peter Bierl, Robin Blackburn, Bianca Bockman, Claire Brill, Melissa Burch, Michael Caplan, Sundrop Carter, Rebecca Carter-Chand, Dan Chodorkoff, Chris Cuomo, Laurel Darlington, Liz DiNovella, Jutta Ditfurth, Christine Dunford, Alison Efford, Paula Emery, Mike Everts, Federico Finchelstein, Marian Firmani, Jessica Flood, Arthur Foelsche, Lauren Fox, Susanne Fries, Grace Gershuny, Paul Glavin, Amy Glaser, Loren Goldner, Gerard Grabowski, Ian Grimmer, Zoltán Grossman, Jane Guskin, Metin Guven, Miriam Hall, Karl Hardy, Howie Hawkins, Ronni Hayon, Jerry Heidenreich, Walter Hergt, Jost Hermand, Matt Hern, Franz Hofer, Barbara Holland-Kunz, Isabel Hull, Wendy Hyman, Harvey Jacobs, David Jimenez, Katie Kadwell, Taran Kang, Ynestra King, Sabina Knight, Gabriel Kuhn, Dominick

LaCapra, Richard Latker, Mary Layoun, Sveinung Legard, Brooke Lehman, Joe Lowndes, Andrea Maihofer, Laura Matthew, Todd May, Metta McGarvey, Carolyn Merchant, Cindy Milstein, Chip Mitchell, Hilary Moore, Chuck Morse, Michelle Moyd, Darini Nicholas, John Nichols, Kate Norlock, Rob Ogman, Mirella Olivari, Kristin Poling, Danny Postel, Michael Premo, Katharina Pühl, Najat Rahman, Sharmila Rudrappa, Allen Ruff, Marsha Rummel, Aaron Sachs, Karl-Ludwig Schibel, Suman Seth, Hilal Sezgin, Jan Shireman, Vic Speedwell, Sophie Statzel, John Staudenmaier, Susie Staudenmaier, Pavlos Stavropoulos, Jim Steakley, Blair Taylor, Eric Toensmeier, Brian Tokar, Laurie Wettstead, Corinne Wilson, Eddie Yuen, Helmut Zander, Peter Zegers, Manfred Zieran, and Laurie Zimmerman. I owe special thanks, above all, to my partner Geeta Raval, who has been my companion and critic throughout.

As I prepared these scattered texts for publication, I was reminded again and again of the singular debt I owe to Murray Bookchin, whose work prefigured the essays presented here. I first met Murray in 1987 and worked with him until his death in 2006. He was famously irascible, and we often disagreed vigorously. But his vision of a principled radical ecological politics and his commitment to a genuinely democratic project of social transformation inspire me still. This book is dedicated to his memory.

Peter Staudenmaier, June 2020

Introduction

Ecofascism Past and Present

Twenty-five years ago, in the summer of 1995, a small book appeared under the title *Ecofascism: Lessons from the German Experience*. It consisted of two essays, one by Janet Biehl on the post-1960s far right and one that I wrote on the so-called "green wing" of the Nazi party. Janet and I had worked together in the Left Green Network and at the Institute for Social Ecology, and both of us had contacts in the radical green milieu in Germany. As we explained in the brief introduction to the volume, we wanted to alert readers to a longstanding but little-known tendency in environmental advocacy, the "hijacking of ecology for racist, nationalistic, and fascist ends." Our goal in examining those trends was to help "preserve the all-important progressive and emancipatory implications of ecological politics."[1]

Over the years since the booklet was first published, the term we chose for our title has taken on a multitude of mutually incompatible meanings, and not a few commentators have preferred to avoid the concept of "ecofascism" altogether. Though an understandable response to widespread confusion about the term, this stance leaves the word open to appropriation by anti-environmental know-nothings as well as far right zealots looking to reclaim their supposedly proud ecological legacy. As long as climate change denial remains the predominant position on much of the established right, particularly in the United States, conservative opponents of environmentalism will exploit historical associations between fascism and ecology in the hopes of discrediting ecological politics as a whole.[2]

In the face of such efforts, then as now, a critical and historically informed engagement with ecofascism as an enduring phenomenon is the only effective alternative. We did not coin the term; it had been circulating on the international left for two decades by the time we borrowed it for the title of our little book.[3] The concept of ecofascism emerged in that distinctive context, among committed left ecologists concerned about the persistence of far right strands of environmentalism.

Despite this background, skepticism toward the notion of ecofascism remains prevalent in some liberal and left quarters. In my view, the concept is best understood as a particular instance of the broader current of right-wing ecology. Since the array of far right, authoritarian, and nationalist politics extends well beyond explicitly fascist forms, a term like "ecofascism" is not the most useful way to refer to all varieties of environmental sentiment on the right. It applies to a specific sub-set of the right, to groups or individuals with both a commitment to ecological issues and active connections to fascist politics. Other forms of reactionary ecological thought can certainly present a serious danger, especially when they involve increasingly aggressive anti-immigrant agitation, but there is little point in labeling them indiscriminately as fascist. The historical specificity of these interlinked traditions makes a difference in how we comprehend them today.[4] For that reason, it can sometimes be more illuminating to refer to "fascist ecology"—the title I gave to my 1995 essay—as the designation for characteristically fascist manifestations of environmental politics.

Whatever its limitations, the term "ecofascism" has become more and more relevant over the past quarter century. Following the horrific attacks in Christchurch and El Paso in 2019, it found renewed public interest and has been critically discussed beyond the English-speaking world.[5] If we want to understand its present relevance, we will need to investigate its history. There have been significant links between environmentalism and right-wing politics for more than a century, in Europe as well as North America and elsewhere, and the fact that ecological concerns were part of classical fascism has been recognized for some time. As Stanley Payne wrote in 1980: "Fascists and Nazis were in fact among the first major environmentalists in twentieth-century politics, though they failed to achieve most of their stipulated goals."[6] Because fascism in general has become more diffuse since 1945, it can be harder to figure out how to apply the concept in today's world.[7] The recent resurgence of the radical right around the globe nonetheless makes it indispensable to face that challenge.

From the 1960s onward there has been a conventional perception that environmental questions are affiliated with the left. Before that, however, ecological matters were much more politically ambivalent, and it was not unusual to find environmental themes on the far right end of the spectrum. From the nineteenth century through the first half of the twentieth, many conservationists in various countries took deeply conservative political positions, often with nationalist and authoritarian features; racist worldviews were common. Knowingly or not, the perpetrators of the Christchurch and El Paso massacres continued that tradition. While they were unusual in putting their beliefs into violent action, many of the same basic ideas run through the contemporary far right scene as well as substantial parts of the political mainstream. Ignoring those uncomfortable facts will not make them go away.

It would be better to take them seriously and confront the challenge they present. For ecological activists who see their work as part of an inclusive liberatory project, this will involve coming to terms with the ambiguous record of environmental politics in historical oscillation between left and right, including the vexed legacy of green trends within fascism. To make sense of the far right's ongoing appeal, we need to take account of its unanticipated facets. Studying the history of right-wing ecology can help contemporary activists learn more about the pitfalls their predecessors encountered and the dilemmas they faced. It can help disentangle current difficulties and provide context for problems that seem inexplicable. It can shed light on apparently paradoxical aspects of green thinking and practice and contribute to a more critical comprehension of current ecological and social crises and the range of responses to them. Conscientious engagement with the convoluted history of environmental politics will strengthen a diverse and radical ecological movement, one that can meet the demands of the present while minding the lessons of the past.

Notes

1   Janet Biehl and Peter Staudenmaier, *Ecofascism: Lessons from the German Experience* (Edinburgh and San Francisco: AK Press, 1995); expanded second edition: Janet Biehl and Peter Staudenmaier, *Ecofascism Revisited: Lessons from the German Experience* (Porsgrunn: New Compass, 2011). Janet Biehl initiated and coordinated the original project and deserves primary credit for it. I remain grateful to her for our cooperation over the years.

2   Examples of the tired environmentalists-are-Nazis genre include Elizabeth Nickson, *Eco-Fascists: How Radical Conservationists Are Destroying Our Natural Heritage* (New York: Broadside, 2012); James Delingpole, *The Little Green Book of Eco-Fascism: The Left's Plan to Frighten Your Kids, Drive Up Energy Costs, and Hike Your Taxes!* (Washington: Regnery, 2014); Rupert Darwall, *Green Tyranny: Exposing the Totalitarian Roots of the Climate Industrial Complex* (New York: Encounter, 2017). Radical rightists, in contrast, have adopted the term "ecofascism" with pride. A recent thread on Stormfront, the chief neo-Nazi online forum in the United States, was titled "Join the Eco-Fascism movement, save our race and planet." Its opening line urged: "Join us Eco-Fascists to bring back nature's balanced order of things." (www.stormfront. org, November 25, 2019) The site hosted previous discussions of "ecofascism" in 2005, 2009, and 2014.

3   See among others André Gorz, *Ecology as Politics* (Boston: South End Press, 1980; French original 1975), which warns against "ecofascism" repeatedly, and the lengthy section titled "Zur realen Gefahr des Öko-Faschismus" in Jan Peters, ed., *Alternativen zum Atomstaat: Das bunte Bild der Grünen* (Berlin: Rotation, 1979), 87-130. Gorz was one of the best known European theorists

of political ecology to emerge from the New Left. Peters came from the vibrant mix of 1970s grassroots movements in West Germany known as the *Bürgerinitiativen* and drew on anti-authoritarian viewpoints; like others from the time, he pointed to the danger of far right appropriation of ecological themes even as he rebuked Stalinist attempts to jump on the green bandwagon. For Murray Bookchin's early use of the term "ecofascism" see e.g. Bookchin, *Toward an Ecological Society* (Montreal: Black Rose, 1980), 277, 309, as well as his 1978 Introduction to "Ecology and Revolutionary Thought" in *Antipode* 10 (1978), 21-22.

4   Matthew Lyons points out: "Conceptual clarity about fascism isn't just an intellectual exercise; it's strategically important for recognizing qualitatively different opponents so we can respond to them intelligently." Lyons, *Insurgent Supremacists: The U.S. Far Right's Challenge to State and Empire* (Oakland: PM Press, 2018), 182.

5   A July 2020 study documented an enormous increase in social media usage of the term "ecofascism," as well as Google searches for the term, from early 2019 onward: Alexander Reid Ross and Emmi Bevensee, "Confronting the Rise of Eco-Fascism" Centre for Analysis of the Radical Right, July 7, 2020. For examples outside of anglophone contexts compare Marco Appel, "El sanguinario resurgimiento del 'ecofascismo'" *Proceso* May 14, 2019; Carlo de Nuzzo and Clémence Pèlegrin, "Les origines historiques de l'écofascisme en Europe" *Le Grand Continent* July 11, 2019; Elsa Koester, "Ökofaschismus: Rechte Ideologen entdecken den Klimaschutz für sich" *Freitag* August 27, 2019; Giusi Palomba, "Ecofascismo rivisitato: Storia e rischi dell'ambientalismo di estrema destra" *Napoli Monitor* March 12, 2020. Numerous further examples are cited in the

following chapters. Entries on "Ecofascism" can be found in a variety of environmental studies handbooks; compare e.g. Dustin Mulvaney, ed., *Green Politics: An A-to-Z Guide* (Los Angeles: Sage, 2011), 116-18; Joni Adamson, ed., *Keywords for Environmental Studies* (New York University Press, 2016), 64-68. As the present volume was being readied for publication, a new article appeared assessing current ecofascist politics in detail: Daniel Rueda, "Neoecofascism: The Example of the United States" *Journal for the Study of Radicalism* 14 (2020), 95-125. Rueda concludes: "Although today it represents a marginal political current, neoecofascism is likely to become increasingly important in the coming years or decades, like other forms of right-wing environmentalism." (116)

6   Stanley Payne, *Fascism: Comparison and Definition* (Madison: University of Wisconsin Press, 1980), 83. Payne also noted that "Hitler was well in advance of his times in his concern about ecology, environmental reform, and pollution." Stanley Payne, *A History of Fascism 1914-1945* (Madison: University of Wisconsin Press, 1995), 204.

7   On the continuing evolution of fascist politics in the "utterly transformed historical landscape" after 1945 see Roger Griffin, *Fascism* (Cambridge: Polity, 2018), 91-125. Scholars, activists, and public intellectuals have yet to settle on a consistent vocabulary for discussing the far right, both because the phenomenon itself is constantly changing and because of ongoing disagreements over proper terminology. In the essays collected in this volume, I have tried to reflect the significant differences among disparate sectors of the right while also recognizing their various points of intersection. In general I use the term "far right" for the broad range of currents examined here, often driven not just

by antagonism toward the left but by an aggrieved contempt for presumedly unwarranted compromise by mainstream conservatives. Within the far right continuum, "radical right" refers to those who take a more aggressively hostile stance against the status quo, demanding greater defiance and intransigence, while "extreme right" refers to those who embrace increasingly belligerent approaches to their perceived enemies, typically culminating in violence. The term "fascism" points to a uniquely toxic apotheosis of all of these elements, forming a historically distinctive family of far right tendencies. Its outlines are traced in the heterogeneous studies by Griffin, Payne, Lyons, and others cited here, which do not offer a consensus about fascism's scale, scope, or fundamental features but nonetheless provide detailed grounds for further analysis.

1.

The Politics of Nature from Left to Right

Radicals, Reactionaries, and
Ecological Responses to Modernity

With his long white hair and flowing robes, Baldur Springmann cut a memorable figure. One of the more colorful spokespeople for the German Greens in their formative years, he was a frequent presence in the West German media during the late 1970s and early 1980s. Viewers who saw him on television then can still recall him decades later. Promoting the Green cause in his idiosyncratic way, Springmann stood out from other leaders of the nascent party. Most of them came from the generation of 1968, the ecological offspring of the radical Sixties. Springmann was much older than his youthful compatriots, and his political roots were decidedly different. Born in 1912, he was a longtime organic farmer whose biodynamic homestead in northern Germany served as a gathering point for environmentalists from the 1950s onward. He worked with pacifist and anti-nuclear groups and was considered one of the pioneers of Germany's ecological movement. Celebratory portraits of him appeared across the spectrum of the German press in 1979 and 1980. From natural farming to alternative spirituality, from organic food to the founding of the Greens, Springmann seemed the very embodiment of modern environmental consciousness.[1]

Baldur Springmann's political involvement did not begin in the democratic context of post-war West Germany, however. His first allegiance was to the Nazi movement, which he joined as a young man shortly after Adolf Hitler came to power in 1933. During the so-called Third Reich, Springmann was a passionate proponent of Nazism's "blood and soil" ideology, combining a mystical reverence for the German peasantry with care for the land they tilled. He worked with other young farmers as part of the Nazi agricultural apparatus. In 1944, a year before the final defeat of the Nazi regime, Springmann wrote a forty-five page manifesto spelling out his "organic-natural" worldview. Its title was taken from a Hitler quotation. The text was based on lectures Springmann presented to German military units as part of the blood and soil propaganda campaign. It remained unpublished and largely escaped the attention of scholars; a typescript copy is stored in an archive in Munich.[2]

Here Springmann railed against "mechanization," "urbanization," and "technological progress," blaming them for "destroying natural communities" and disrupting "the organic harmony of body, soul, and spirit." While the rest of the world wallowed in industrial defilement, Nazi Germany alone offered the last chance for salvaging "the eternal rhythms of nature." Centuries of rural peasant life on German soil, close to the earth, had produced a "natural elite" marked by "Nordic blood." This "organic living order," however, was gravely threatened by Germany's enemies: the Americans, the Bolsheviks, the "Polacks," and other racial inferiors. But the most pernicious enemy of all was "the Jews," who were nothing more than "flies on the body of humankind." With their "degenerate intellect," the Jews had subjugated most of the planet and were now in danger of "enslaving" the German people as well. The only hope was for all Germans to support the Führer and his "war for freedom." Once free of the Jewish yoke, Germany would be able to return to its rightful inheritance of peaceful communities growing healthy food on their own soil.

What would Springmann's comrades in the Greens have thought if they had known about this part of his past? He didn't stay long enough to find out. In 1981 Springmann quit the Green party because it had moved too far to the left, in his view, embracing social causes that did not fit his image of a natural order. He later accused the Greens of "anti-Germanism."[3] With a group of like-minded former Greens, Springmann went on to found a series of small right-wing environmental organizations.[4] He increasingly associated himself with esoteric and neo-pagan spiritual currents. By his death in 2003 he had drifted to the extreme right margins of German society. Far right environmental advocates continue to invoke his legacy today.[5] Spanning the troubled twentieth century, Springmann's strange career exemplified the historical contradictions built into the politics of nature in the modern world.

Eccentric as he was, it would be easy to dismiss Baldur Springmann as an aberration, a random erstwhile Nazi who happened to wander into the Greens' orbit. But he was hardly alone. Other far right figures, some with equally extensive Nazi backgrounds, were involved in the early years of the German Greens.[6] As the movement matured, left activists within the Greens successfully sidelined their would-be counterparts on the right by linking ecological themes to an emancipatory social vision while rejecting notions of purity and natural order. Nazism's blood and soil heritage forced the young party to face the profound political ambivalence of ecology. For the most part, though, the convoluted history of the politics of nature remained a minor theme, unacknowledged and unresolved, a dynamic that is all too common when the past meets the present.[7]

The problem is by no means unique to the German Greens. It arises any time ecological concerns take political form. All varieties of environmentalism eventually sort out, implicitly or explicitly, what they draw from the left and from the right as well as the emergent space between those poles. Green parties may be famous for claiming a lineage that is "neither left nor right," but that formulation—assuming it is more than mere public relations rhetoric—typically reveals political confusion and historical naïveté rather than substantive innovation. Since the nineteenth century, environmental issues have functioned as an intermediary for social discontent, a register of the uncertainties and misgivings that modern societies continually generate.

Whether refracted through categories of class, race, gender, nation, religion, science, and so forth, or in the more diffuse mode that characterizes many reform currents in the Global North, the politics of nature offers a way for individuals and communities alike to navigate the precarious terrain of modern life and search for alternatives.

This is what gives ecological challenges their powerful potential to spark fundamental social change. But it can also expose an unmistakable sense of political disorientation. The depth and severity of the environmental crises we face seem to disrupt conventional political concepts, revealing them as utterly inadequate to the task of comprehending our current predicament. Perhaps the two most confounding structures that underlie this constant sense of disorientation are the twin institutional pillars of modernity: capitalism and the state.[8] For those of us on the radical left, the struggle against these structures has seemingly always been a part of our history, whether in socialist, anarchist, feminist, or communalist form. What we too often forget is that the same is true for the history of the right, including the far right. This is particularly the case with capitalism, often considered primarily responsible for contemporary ecological destruction. In our attempts to make sense of the modern crisis, we would do well to take a closer look at the strikingly broad range of responses that the rise of capitalism has produced, responses that extend across the entire political spectrum.[9]

Even Baldur Springmann, in his 1944 manifesto, denounced the depredations of capitalism with its drive for profit and continual commodification of the natural world, an artificial system that reduced farmers to "grain manufacturers" and "milk suppliers" instead of caretakers for the soil. Springmann blamed all this on Jewish "financial magnates" who had usurped the proper place of hard-working Germans and their sacred bond with the land.[10] Other Nazi supporters of organic farming shared Springmann's views on this well-worn theme, condemning "speculative capitalism" and its Jewish overlords for ruining German agriculture.[11] They claimed that the chemical fertilizer industry was controlled by "Jewish finance capital" and that the degradation of German soil was the fault of "the Jewish masters of the banks and stock markets."[12] Indeed "capitalism itself," they insisted, was the nefarious invention of "international Jewry."[13]

The conflation of capitalism with Jews is one of the perennial hallmarks of right-wing critiques of capitalism, though it has repeatedly appeared in left contexts as well. It is a way of personalizing capitalism, making an opaque and abstract economic system seem more concrete and comprehensible by associating it with an identifiable group. Nazi antisemitism drew extensively on this illusion of concreteness and immediacy.[14] It is always tempting to believe that a highly complex social system can be simplified into a straightforward story of good guys and bad guys. It is even more tempting when these stories are cast in terms of an idyllic vision of restored nature.

Such simplifications were not, of course, peculiar to Nazi Germany. The phenomenon that Dan Stone has aptly labeled "rural revivalism" could be found in a number of interwar European societies, frequently linking racial and agrarian concerns.[15] Organic farming was a conspicuously common feature of these right-wing utopias not just in Germany but in Britain, North America, and elsewhere. This troubling fact serves as a reminder of the extent to which the "environmentalist tradition" has historically been "bound up with the radical right."[16] Even in Fascist Italy, scarcely a model of ecological practice, environmental policies consistently linked landscape, race, and ruralism.[17] Fascist ideologues, like their Nazi counterparts, celebrated "the power of race, the cult of the soil, the agrarian tradition."[18] Italian ecologists credited Mussolini with the "rebirth of the nation's forests."[19] Ideas like these were widespread on the European right at the time. During the 1930s, Hitler's admirers abroad praised Nazi Germany for its "back-to-the-land" efforts and its "assault on urbanisation and industrialism."[20]

It can be hard to reconcile such factors with the conventional image of fascism and the far right. Yet these findings are not new. Forty years ago George Mosse observed that fascism in its disparate varieties presents itself as "a door into a utopia of tolerance, of happiness, of productivity, and all the things that people long for." Nazism, Mosse wrote, "promised a future outside the problems of industrialization, outside the problems of urbanization."[21] This promise ultimately proved hollow, but that did not render it less appealing to millions of people in the wake of the First World War and the Great Depression. What makes these insights provocative is their disconcerting proximity to longstanding arguments on the radical left and among progressive ecological activists. That is why it is important to understand the politically fraught history of ecological responses to the failures of modern society in its capitalist and statist form.

One way to begin that process of understanding is to attempt the difficult task of distinguishing left versions of ecological politics from right versions. Any effort along those lines faces several vexing problems. The same features that make definition and categorization useful conceptual tools—simplicity, clarity, precision—are unfortunately ill-suited to the messiness of social life. Historical reality in all its complexity does not fit easily into convenient ideal types. Nevertheless, it may be worth venturing an initial broad distinction between two tentatively outlined kinds, what we might call radical and reactionary responses to modernity. Consider the example of capitalism, viewed through the lens of a provisional differentiation: Reactionary critiques of capitalism reflect a nostalgic vision of returning to a simpler and wholesome communal life undisturbed by the demands of the modern world. Radical critiques of capitalism, in contrast, embody an emancipatory outlook that strives to create new social forms, indeed an entirely new society, in order to transcend the shortcomings of capitalist modernity without rejecting the modern project as such. This preliminary attempt at classification is undoubtedly much too simplistic, but it can serve as a fruitful starting point, to be refined and revised as necessary.

Unsurprisingly, many real-world responses to the ravages of capitalism do not fall neatly into either the radical or the reactionary camp. This is especially true for environmentalist responses. Some of the most popular models in European and North American environmental circles represent a hybrid of left and right strands. Several of them center on panaceas and facile solutions, such as Henry George's single tax proposals or the Social Credit movement founded by C.

H. Douglas. Others offer full-fledged alternative economic visions like Rudolf Steiner's "threefold commonwealth" or Silvio Gesell's "natural economic order." Though their roots lie in the nineteenth century, these models still find admirers in twenty-first century radical quarters.[22] In many ways, however, their assumptions and implications are firmly reactionary, as left critics have pointed out.[23] The case of the Social Credit movement is perhaps the most striking; Douglas explicitly based his economic theories on the infamous antisemitic forgery "The Protocols of the Elders of Zion."[24]

It is crucial to keep this historical background in mind when we look at figures like Baldur Springmann, either in the 1940s or the 1980s, or when we encounter comparable environmental advocates today. Modern capitalism is an extremely complicated system that resists easy explanation. It isn't shocking that many ostensibly alternative proposals fall short in attempting to make sense of an apparently senseless economic arrangement. But it is important to pay attention to the patterns that arise in such foreshortened critiques of capitalism, which frequently mistake symptoms for structural causes. They typically end up focused on the superficial, decrying the most visible and most distressing aspects of life under capitalism rather than examining its underlying systemic forces. Foreshortened critiques of capitalism also tend to reproduce a series of seductively simple dichotomies, such as productive versus parasitic, local versus global, and concrete versus abstract, that sometimes seem radical but have historically had reactionary consequences.

For those on the left who seek to build a life after capitalism and are working toward an ecological society, the vital lesson is this: We are not the only anti-capitalists out there—not historically, and not today. The discontent and dislocation that capitalism systematically produces can spin off in myriad directions, and many of them are emphatically not emancipatory; they do not point toward freedom, equality, or environmental flourishing. They can just as readily undermine the very values and practices we are fighting for. In societies distorted by capitalism and the state, anxieties and unrest aimed at the status quo are always double-edged. If we hope they will lead to more democracy, participation, cooperation, and egalitarianism, toward a world that is ecologically vibrant and socially dynamic, we will need to think carefully about how we respond to the ambiguities of environmental politics.

As much as we might wish otherwise, Baldur Springmann's incongruous sojourn with the German Greens was not, at bottom, an anomaly. At times this has proven confusing for those expecting a clear-cut tale of environmental heroes and villains. It is not unusual for left critics of right-wing ecological politics to be mistaken for enemies of environmentalism as such.[25] The fact that such mistakes continue to recur after several decades of efforts by left ecologists to clarify the arguments at stake—arguments that matter deeply to the future of environmentalism in whatever form—indicates just how perplexing the subject remains, historically as well as politically. It is an invitation to take a closer look at a topic that many would prefer to avoid.

Springmann and his ilk were not merely rustic oddballs. They stood for a brand of environmental politics that has persisted for over a hundred years. Far from disappearing in

1945, it has continued to arouse interest and attract adherents across the globe. Significant portions of the post-war organic farming movement, from Australia to Britain to France, were affiliated with far right politics.[26] Italian neo-fascists in the 1970s were eagerly interested in "ecology, macrobiotics, and alternative medicine," sponsoring green workshops and publishing a magazine titled *Environmental Dimension*.[27] Their confederates in the Spanish and French radical right shared "a keen interest in environmentalism," while "ecologism" was a core principle for parts of the extreme right in the Netherlands in the 1980s.[28] In contemporary Germany the so-called "New Right" has appropriated ecology as one of its favored causes.[29] In 2017 Marine Le Pen, leader of the far right National Front, presented an environmental agenda promoting organic agriculture and demanding a zero-carbon economy in France. She called for a "revolution in eating locally" and excoriated multinational corporations for pushing genetically modified crops and "poisoning the land" with pesticides.[30] It would be easier to dismiss such episodes as hollow campaign rhetoric if the overall trend were not so pronounced.

White supremacist organizations in the United States today still espouse a vision of blood and soil. "Vanguard America," one of several groups active in the current resurgence of the extreme right, ran the website "bloodandsoil.org" until it was taken down after the August 2017 events in Charlottesville, Virginia.[31] Their manifesto, adorned with fascist imagery, declared the Unites States "a nation exclusively for the White

American peoples" and called for "an America based on the immutable truths of Blood and Soil." It warned that "the large multinational corporations that have bled this nation dry will not be allowed to continue their detrimental efforts unabated." The manifesto avowed:

> America must be once again built from the ground up to recapture the glory an Aryan nation deserves. Vanguard America stands indomitably opposed to the tyranny of globalism and capitalism, a system under which nations are stripped of their heritage and their people are turned into nothing more than units of cheap, expendable labor. [...] A nation based upon the values of self-reliance and fellowship must be created which stands entirely apart from the dictatorship of international finance. Like all independent nations, America should strive for a truly national economy. An economy that is self-contained, and free from the influence of international corporations, led by a rootless group of international Jews, which place profit beyond the interests of our people, or any people.

Proclamations like these reveal the worldview that animates reactionary responses to a distorted modernity. Their historical origins are not confined to the extreme right, but extend to mainstream environmentalism as well. The roots of the American conservation movement have long been entangled with various outgrowths of racism, eugenics, and xenophobia.[32]

But we are not bound to repeat the mistakes of the past. We can learn from those mistakes as we reach toward a better world. This will mean taking seriously the lengthy tradition of right-wing environmental politics, and facing it squarely, rather than pretending that this tradition is a minor deviation from an otherwise proud history. "Ecological discourse," as one scholar has noted, "forms a major constituent of right-wing thought."[33] Today as before, the emancipatory potential of the ecology movement is threatened with eclipse by a sadly familiar assortment of reactionary and authoritarian forms of ecological thinking.

The 2019 attacks in Christchurch and El Paso were a stark warning that the links between environmental sentiment and anti-immigrant ideology are becoming more virulent on the right: mass murder rationalized through ecological claims. Explaining their heinous acts, the El Paso shooter condemned "the destruction of our environment" while the Christchurch shooter proclaimed himself an "eco-fascist."[34] In the aftermath of these atrocities, there is a strong tendency to dismiss the perpetrators as aberrant and their beliefs as marginal. When the same beliefs are repeatedly invoked to justify homicidal violence, however, it is all the more imperative to confront their history.

That will not be an easy undertaking. Reckoning conscientiously with the mercurial politics of environmentalism raises far-reaching questions. Capitalism and the state, after all, are not the only social structures that shape modern life. Radical ecologists also contend with the legacy of patriarchy and white supremacy, which are just as important—for opposite reasons—to the far right. Racial and sexual hierarchies have long claimed natural status as their justification, another variation on the politics of nature. They have also left their mark on the evolution of environmentalism.[35] Along with the colonial origins of conservation and similarly neglected elements, these controversies await broader informed and incisive engagement.

All of this means we have more work to do. A critical reassessment of environmental responses to the predicaments of modern society will require difficult choices about political practice. We do not have to settle for approaches that preach personal change in place of social change or that promise an untarnished refuge from the burdens of history. We do not have to accept an environmentalism that ignores its ancestry. We can ask for much more radical possibilities. If environmental politics have historically been susceptible to the authoritarian right, perhaps ecological activists today would do well to align themselves with the anti-authoritarian left.

A hard look at the politics of nature leaves us with as many questions as answers. It is not just a matter of examining our ideas or altering our thinking; as Carolyn Merchant reminds us: "A new story can be written only through human action."[36] Ecological activists face a daunting array of challenges, and many other issues demand our attention. This can make attending to our own history seem self-indulgent. But it is part of our responsibility to the future. Any candid process of political discernment can be trying, and some will find the very idea divisive and distasteful. That is why it deserves honest reflection and forthright debate. As we steer our way through the general crisis of the twenty-first century, we will be wise to keep in mind the wrong turns taken in the past.

Notes

1   Makoto Nishida, *Strömungen in den Grünen (1980-2003): Eine
    Analyse über informell-organisierte Gruppen innerhalb der Grünen*
    (Münster: Lit, 2005), 38-43; Frank Schnieder, *Von der sozialen
    Bewegung zur Institution? Die Entstehung der Partei Die Grünen
    in den Jahren 1978 bis 1980* (Münster: Lit, 1998), 42-45, 113-
    15; Silke Mende, *"Nicht rechts, nicht links, sondern vorn": Eine
    Geschichte der Gründungsgrünen* (Munich: Oldenbourg, 2011),
    244-49. Mende cites 1979-80 articles about Springmann from the
    Frankfurter Allgemeine Zeitung, Die Zeit, Stern, Bild, and a variety
    of other organs; he was also featured in the *Spiegel* and elsewhere
    as well. See additionally the obituary for Springmann in the
    tageszeitung October 25, 2003.

2   Baldur Springmann, "Das Deutsche Reich wird ein Bauernreich
    sein" Institut für Zeitgeschichte ED 643/1.

3   1995 interview with Springmann in *Junge Freiheit* quoted in
    Jonathan Olsen, *Nature and Nationalism: Right-Wing Ecology
    and the Politics of Identity in Contemporary Germany* (New York:
    St. Martin's Press, 1999), 50. Olsen fittingly characterizes *Junge
    Freiheit* at the time as a "radical right wing" journal.

4   Compare Volkmar Wölk, *Natur und Mythos:
    Ökologiekonzeptionen der 'Neuen' Rechten im Spannungsfeld
    zwischen Blut und Boden und New Age* (Duisburg: Institut für
    Sprach- und Sozialforschung, 1992); Oliver Geden, *Rechte
    Ökologie: Umweltschutz zwischen Emanzipation und Faschismus*
    (Berlin: Elefanten, 1996); Jutta Ditfurth, *Das waren die Grünen:
    Abschied von einer Hoffnung* (Munich: Econ, 2000); Peter Bierl,
    Grüne Braune: Umwelt-, Tier- und Heimatschutz von rechts
    (Münster: Unrast, 2014).

5   Anke Oxenfarth, ed., *Ökologie von rechts: Braune Umweltschützer auf Stimmenfang* (Munich: Oekom, 2012), 21; Gudrun Heinrich, ed., *Naturschutz und Rechtsradikalismus: Gegenwärtige Entwicklungen, Probleme, Abgrenzungen* (Bonn: Bundesamt für Naturschutz, 2015), 121, 128.

6   The better known examples include Werner Vogel (1907-1992) and Werner Haverbeck (1909-1999). For further context see Richard Stöss, *Vom Nationalismus zum Umweltschutz* (Opladen: Westdeutscher Verlag, 1980); Peter Dudek, "Konservatismus, Rechtsextremismus und die 'Philosophie der Grünen'" in Thomas Kluge, ed., *Grüne Politik: Der Stand der Auseinandersetzung* (Frankfurt: Fischer, 1984), 90-108; Margret Feit, *Die "Neue Rechte" in der Bundesrepublik: Organisation, Ideologie, Strategie* (Frankfurt: Campus, 1987), 151-56; Justus Ulbricht, "Grün als Brücke zu Braun: Über die Schwierigkeiten der Ökologiebewegung mit dem rechten Rand" *Politische Ökologie* 11 (1993), 7-12; Alison Statham, "Ecology and the German Right" in Colin Riordan, ed., *Green Thought in German Culture: Historical and Contemporary Perspectives* (Cardiff: University of Wales Press, 1997), 125-38; as well as the valuable selection of material from the 1970s collected in Jan Peters, ed., *Nationaler "Sozialismus" von rechts* (Berlin: Guhl, 1980) and Jan Peters, *Rechtsextremisten als Umweltschützer* (Berlin: Freunde der Erde, 1980).

7   In a thoughtful and self-critical retrospective interview, a leader of one of the left currents within the early Greens, eco-socialist Thomas Ebermann, acknowledged that he and his comrades underestimated the potential for far-right appropriation of ecology: Ebermann in Michael Schroeren, ed., *Die Grünen* (Vienna: Ueberreuter, 1990), 219-20.

8   For an argument that capitalism and the nation state form the

central institutions of modernity see Robert Marks, *The Origins of the Modern World* (Lanham: Rowman & Littlefield, 2015). Though the examples I draw on in this essay come from Western contexts, it is essential to recognize that comparable dynamics mark the history of the Global South as well; see the analysis of anti-colonial intellectuals as early "critics of modernity" in Pankaj Mishra, *From the Ruins of Empire: The Revolt Against the West and the Remaking of Asia* (London: Picador, 2012), 302.

9   On the contours of "the modern crisis," along with its alternative potentials and its "hidden message of freedom," see Murray Bookchin, *The Modern Crisis* (Philadelphia: New Society Publishers, 1986). Despite its many problems, the notoriously vague term "modernity" can sometimes help discern key aspects of the plight we face. It has become common in discussions of the history of environmentalism: "the rise of ecological holism in Europe and North America throughout the twentieth century helped mitigate the spiritual and existential disorientation of modernity." Frank Zelko, "'A Flower Is Your Brother!' Holism, Nature, and the (Non-ironic) Enchantment of Modernity" *Intellectual History Review* 23 (2013), 517-36, quote on 518. For broader perspective see Ramachandra Guha, *Environmentalism: A Global History* (New York: Longman, 2000).

10 These ideas have a lengthy history. As George Kren noted decades ago: "This rootlessness came more and more to dominate the evolving stereotype of the Jew. Thus, by the nineteenth century they were associated with the city, were accused of lacking roots in soil and country, of being rationally calculating and without feeling,—and above all of lacking the German's reverence for the higher things in life. This is the central theme of what is probably the most famous German anti-Semitic novel of the nineteenth

century, Wilhelm von Polenz's *Der Büttnerbauer*, first published in 1895. This work contrasts the honest, simple German peasant, tied to the soil, with the rootless urban Jew. Stating a theme which National Socialism was to reemphasize, Polenz described the Jew as a person lacking any appreciation of the mystical qualities of inherited land, and contrasts him to the honest, simple German peasant with firm and deep roots in the sacred inherited land. In the novel the Jew lends the peasant money at usury and the latter, unable to repay it, loses the land to the Jew who, without regard for the true purpose of the soil, builds a factory on it. The peasant, unable to bear this sacrilege, hangs himself on an old tree on the land." Kren, "Race and Ideology" *Phylon* 23 (1962), 167-77.

11 Georg Halbe, "Zur neuen Getreideordnung" *Deutschlands Erneuerung: Monatsschrift für das deutsche Volk,* September 1934, 552-56. Halbe was an energetic proponent of biodynamic farming within the Nazi agricultural apparatus. He oversaw the "Blut und Boden Verlag," the party's "Blood and Soil" publishing house. Beginning in 1942 he worked for the Ministry for the Occupied Eastern Territories. He also published in the journal of the biodynamic movement; see Georg Halbe, "Goethes Naturanschauung und lebensgesetzlicher Landbau" *Demeter* December 1940, 116-18.

12 Hermann Schneider, *Unser täglich Brot: Lebensfragen der deutschen Landwirtschaft* (Munich: Nationalsozialistische Bibliothek, 1930), 41, 72. Alongside antisemitic tirades, the pamphlet—published under Nazi auspices—makes a strong case for organic farming methods. Like Halbe, Schneider (1872-1953) was an early Nazi supporter of biodynamic agriculture. He joined the party in 1929 and served as a Nazi member of the Reichstag from 1930 onward, soon becoming a prominent agricultural official for the

party and the SS. Schneider remained an outspoken advocate of biodynamics throughout the Nazi era; see e.g. Hermann Schneider, *Schicksalsgemeinschaft Europa: Leben und Nahrung aus der europäischen Scholle* (Breslau: Gutsmann, 1941).

13 Günther Pacyna, *Der deutsche Bauer im Osten* (Berlin: Engelhard, 1943), 137. Pacyna was yet another supporter of biodynamic farming in the Nazi agricultural apparatus. The role of the biodynamic movement in the Nazi era has received increasing attention in historical scholarship. As a recent overview notes, "The natural farming system that undoubtedly generated the most excitement and support within Nazi circles was biodynamics." Corinna Treitel, *Eating Nature in Modern Germany: Food, Agriculture and Environment, c. 1870-2000* (Cambridge: Cambridge University Press, 2017), 213. Another study points out: "numerous documents provide evidence that the organization of farming processes and daily work schedules to agree with biodynamic principles supported by parts of the SS power apparatus was taken very seriously." Willi Oberkrome, "National Socialist Blueprints for Rural Communities and their Resonance in Agrarian Society" in Martina Steber, ed., *Visions of Community in Nazi Germany* (Oxford: Oxford University Press, 2014), 270-80, quote on 273.

14 Moishe Postone, "Anti-Semitism and National Socialism" *New German Critique* 19 (1980), 97-115. For background compare Christine Achinger and Marcel Stoetzler, "German Modernity, Barbarous Slavs and Profit-seeking Jews" *Nations and Nationalism* 19 (2013), 739-60; Bernd Sommer, "Anti-capitalism in the name of ethno-nationalism: ideological shifts on the German extreme right" *Patterns of Prejudice* 42 (2008), 305-16; Pierre Birnbaum, "Anti-Semitism and Anticapitalism in Modern France" in Frances Malino and Bernard Wasserstein, eds., *The Jews in Modern France*

(Hanover: University Press of New England, 1985), 214-23; Heike Hoffmann, "Völkische Kapitalismus-Kritik" in Uwe Puschner, ed., *Handbuch zur 'Völkischen Bewegung' 1871-1918* (Munich: Saur, 1996), 558-71; Matthew Lange, *Antisemitic Elements in the Critique of Capitalism in German Culture, 1850-1933* (Oxford: Lang, 2007); Nicolas Berg, ed., *Kapitalismusdebatten um 1900: Über antisemitisierende Semantiken des Jüdischen* (Leipzig: Leipziger Universitätsverlag, 2011); Michael Barthel and Benjamin Jung, *Völkischer Antikapitalismus? Eine Einführung in die Kapitalismuskritik von rechts* (Münster: Unrast, 2013); Robert Ogman, *Against the Nation: Anti-National Politics in Germany* (Porsgrunn: New Compass, 2013); Michele Battini, *Socialism of Fools: Capitalism and Modern Anti-Semitism* (New York: Columbia University Press, 2016).

15 Dan Stone, "Rural Revivalism and the Radical Right in France and Britain between the Wars" in Stone, *The Holocaust, Fascism and Memory* (New York: Palgrave Macmillan, 2013), 110-22.

16 Stone, "Rural Revivalism and the Radical Right," 115. In a searching reflection on "the Holocaust as an ecological project," the late Boaz Neumann argued that "politically the modern ecological idea originates from the conservative Right." Boaz Neumann, "National Socialism, Holocaust, and Ecology" in Dan Stone, ed., *The Holocaust and Historical Methodology* (Oxford: Berghahn, 2012), 101-23, quote on 104.

17 Marco Armiero and Wilko Graf von Hardenberg, "Green Rhetoric in Blackshirts: Italian Fascism and the Environment" *Environment and History* 19 (2013), 283-311. A standard history of Fascism observes: "One of the most unique features of the Italian regime in its own time was its emphasis on ecology, on the *ridimensionamento* of national socioeconomic structure, which

aimed at controlling urbanization, improving environmental conditions, promoting reforestation, and keeping a large percentage of the rural population in the countryside." Stanley Payne, *A History of Fascism 1914-1945* (Madison: University of Wisconsin Press, 1995), 478.

18 Massimo Scaligero, "La razza, la terra e il fuoco" *La Vita Italiana* December 1941, 626-30.

19 Aldo Pavari, "The Fascist Government and the Restoration of Italian Forests" *Forestry* 8 (1934), 67-75.

20 Anthony Ludovici, "Hitler and the Third Reich" *English Review* September 1936, 231-39.

21 George Mosse, *Nazism: A Historical and Comparative Analysis of National Socialism* (New Brunswick: Transaction, 1978), 34, 40.

22 A conspicuous example is the article by conspiracy theorist Guido Preparata, "Perishable Money in a Threefold Commonwealth: Rudolf Steiner and the Social Economics of an Anarchist Utopia" *Review of Radical Political Economics* 38 (2006), 619-48. Preparata is a fan of Silvio Gesell and C. H. Douglas as well as Steiner. For earlier statements from Steiner's and Gesell's followers see Owen Barfield, "The Relation between the Economics of C.H. Douglas and those of Rudolf Steiner" *Anthroposophy: A Quarterly Review of Spiritual Science*, September 1933, 272-85; Heinrich Nidecker, *Gesundung des sozialen Organismus nach den Vorschlägen von Rudolf Steiner und Silvio Gesell* (Bern: Pestalozzi-Fellenberg-Haus, 1926); Werner Onken, "Silvio Gesell und Rudolf Steiner: Wegbereiter einer sozialen Zukunft" *Fragen der Freiheit* January 1990, 4-38.

23 See e.g. Derek Wall, "Social Credit: The Ecosocialism of Fools" *Capitalism Nature Socialism* 14 (2003), 99-122; Robert Kurz, "Politische Ökonomie des Antisemitismus" *Krisis* 17 (1995), 177-218; Peter Bierl, *Schwundgeld, Freiwirtschaft und Rassenwahn.*

Kapitalismuskritk von rechts: Der Fall Silvio Gesell (Hamburg: Konkret, 2012); Mark Loeffler, "Populists and Parasites: On Producerist Reason" in John Abromeit, ed., *Transformations of Populism in Europe and the Americas* (London: Bloomsbury Academic, 2017), 265-92. For historical context on Rudolf Steiner's "threefold commonwealth" teachings see Helmut Zander, *Anthroposophie in Deutschland: Theosophische Weltanschauung und gesellschaftliche Praxis 1884–1945* (Göttingen: Vandenhoeck & Ruprecht, 2007), 1239-1356; Peter Staudenmaier, *Between Occultism and Nazism: Anthroposophy and the Politics of Race in the Fascist Era* (Leiden: Brill, 2014), 64-100.

24 C. H. Douglas, *Social Credit* (London: Palmer, 1924), 11, 56-59. See also C.B. Macpherson, *Democracy in Alberta: Social Credit and the Party System* (Toronto: University of Toronto Press, 1962); Bob Hesketh, *Major Douglas and Alberta Social Credit* (Toronto: University of Toronto Press, 1997); Janine Stingel, *Social Discredit: Anti-Semitism, Social Credit, and the Jewish Response* (Montreal: McGill-Queen's University Press, 2000).

25 A personal example may help illustrate the problem. A few years ago, in an online review, a fellow professor of history denounced a book that I had co-authored, characterizing it as an "anti-ecology tome" founded on "right-wing political bias." The book in question was Janet Biehl and Peter Staudenmaier, *Ecofascism Revisited* (New Compass Press, 2011), originally published in 1995. Readers who take a brief look at either edition of the book will quickly see that it is a left-wing critique of right-wing tendencies, not the other way around. The review was later retracted, but the incident is nonetheless quite illuminating. When even professional historians can't tell left from right, we have a lot more work to do in order to make sense of the politics of nature.

26 Andrea Gaynor, "Antipodean Eco-nazis? The Organic Gardening and Farming Movement and Far-right Ecology in Postwar Australia" *Australian Historical Studies* 43 (2012), 253-69; Venus Bivar, *Organic Resistance: The Struggle over Industrial Farming in Postwar France* (Chapel Hill: University of North Carolina Press, 2018), 50-72. On "overt fascist sympathies" in the early British organic movement see Gregory Barton, *The Global History of Organic Farming* (Oxford: Oxford University Press, 2018), 134, 21, 30, 157-59. For the German case see Corinna Treitel, "Artificial or Biological? Nature, Fertilizer, and the German Origins of Organic Agriculture" in Denise Phillips and Sharon Kingsland, eds., *New Perspectives on the History of Life Sciences and Agriculture* (London: Springer, 2015), 183-203.

27 Marco Tarchi, *La rivoluzione impossibile: Dai Campi Hobbit alla Nuova destra* (Florence: Vallecchi, 2010), 223-27; Mario Bozzi Sentieri, *Dal neofascismo alla nuova destra* (Rome: Nuove Idee, 2007), 201-05. For further neo-fascist discussions of "ecology," "urbanization," and "industrial congestion" in the 1970s see Mauro Lenci, *A destra, oltre la destra: La cultura politica del neofascismo italiano, 1945-1995* (Pisa: Pisa University Press, 2012), 39; Piero Ignazi, *Il polo escluso: Profilo storico del Movimento Sociale Italiano* (Bologna: Il Mulino, 1998), 190-91. An incisive analysis of this milieu can be found in Furio Jesi, *Cultura di destra* (Milan: Garzanti, 1993). The trend was not peculiar to Italy: "Even as the German revolutionary nationalists joined the environmentalist movement in the late 1970s, the Spanish radical far right made a specialty of setting up environmental and anti-speciesist associations." Jean-Yves Camus and Nicolas Lebourg, *Far-Right Politics in Europe* (Cambridge: Harvard University Press, 2017), 86.

28 Camus and Lebourg, *Far-Right Politics in Europe*, 45, 86, 131, 216; Cas Mudde, *The Ideology of the Extreme Right* (Manchester: Manchester University Press, 2002), 158-59.

29 For a representative example see Norbert Borrmann, "Ökologie ist rechts" *Sezession* October 2013, 4-7, part of a special issue of the journal devoted to ecology. This is not just a theoretical interest; the German far right has taken a markedly hands-on approach to environmental concerns. See Kate Connolly, "German far-right extremists tap into green movement for support" *Guardian* April 28, 2012; Sally McGrane, "The Right-Wing Organic Farmers of Germany" *New Yorker* January 11, 2013; Christian Thiele and Marlene Weiss, "Unterwanderung des Biolandbaus durch Rechtsextreme" *Süddeutsche Zeitung* April 13, 2012; Ann-Kathrin Hoffmann, *Zwischen braunem Sumpf und grüner Idylle* (Ökologischer Bundesfreiwilligendienst 2014). Similar forms of ideological disorientation can be found on the left as well; see e.g. Marko Ferst, ed., *Wege zur ökologischen Zeitenwende* (Berlin: Zeitsprung, 2002). For critical context cf. Peter Thompson, "New Age Mysticism, Postmodernism and Human Liberation" in Riordan, ed., *Green Thought in German Culture*, 107-24.

30 Michael Stothard, "Marine Le Pen uses environmental issue to broaden appeal" *Financial Times* January 26, 2017. For earlier French examples see the September 1993 issue of the "New Right" journal *Krisis* dedicated to ecology; for current comparison see Giovanni Monastra and Philippe Baillet, *Piété pour le cosmos: Les précurseurs antimodernes de l'écologie profonde* (Saint-Genis-Laval: Éditions Akribeia, 2017).

31 I copied the text of the "Vanguard America" manifesto from their "bloodandsoil.org" website in April 2017. As of March 2018 that website hosted a group calling itself "Patriot Front," which split

off from "Vanguard America" in September 2017. The "Patriot Front" site inveighs against "the encroaching rot of modernism" and a society that has become "utterly detached from nature." It calls for "a people free from the vices of the modern world" who are to be "removed from decadence and given community." Many strands on the right avail themselves of this ideological ensemble; see the recent survey by Peter Kolozi, *Conservatives Against Capitalism: From the Industrial Revolution to Globalization* (New York: Columbia University Press, 2017). For comparison with antisemitic themes in left contexts see the perceptive analyses by Robert Fine and Philip Spencer, *Antisemitism and the left: On the return of the Jewish question* (Manchester: Manchester University Press, 2017); Sina Arnold, "From Occupation to Occupy: Antisemitism and the Contemporary Left in the United States" in Alvin Rosenfeld, ed., *Deciphering the New Antisemitism* (Bloomington: Indiana University Press, 2015), 375-404; Dominique Miething, "Antisemitism in the anarchist tradition" *Anarchist Studies* 26 (2018), 105-08.

32 Compare Carolyn Merchant, "Shades of Darkness: Race and Environmental History" *Environmental History* 8 (2003), 380-94; Jade Sasser, "From Darkness into Light: Race, Population, and Environmental Advocacy" *Antipode* 46 (2014), 1240-57; Garland Allen, "'Culling the Herd': Eugenics and the Conservation Movement in the United States, 1900–1940" *Journal of the History of Biology* 46 (2013), 31-72; Jedediah Purdy, "Environmentalism's Racist History" *New Yorker* August 13, 2015; Lisa Sun-Hee Park and David Naguib Pellow, "Nativism and the Environmental Movement" in *The Slums of Aspen: Immigrants vs. the Environment in America's Eden* (New York: New York University Press, 2011), 127-61; Carl Zimring, *Clean and White: A History of*

Environmental Racism in the United States (New York: New York University Press, 2016).

33 Statham, "Ecology and the German Right," 129. She also points to "a strong element of convergence in rhetoric between right and left" on environmental issues (134). Compare Jonathan Olsen, "The Perils of Rootedness: On Bioregionalism and Right Wing Ecology in Germany" *Landscape Journal* 19 (2000), 73-83; Tamara Mix, "The Greening of White Separatism: Use of Environmental Themes to Elaborate and Legitimize Extremist Discourse" *Nature & Culture* 4 (2009), 138-66; Mi Park, "The trouble with eco-politics of localism: Too close to the far right?" *Interface* 5 (2013), 318-43; Madeleine Hurd and Steffen Werther, "The Militant Media of Neo-Nazi Environmentalism" in Heike Graf, ed., *The Environment in the Age of the Internet* (Cambridge: Open Book, 2016), 137-70. A recently published volume offers contemporary international perspectives: Bernhard Forchtner, ed., *The Far Right and the Environment: Politics, Discourse and Communication* (London: Routledge, 2019).

34 This essay was originally written in early 2018, before the attacks in Pittsburgh, Christchurch, El Paso, and elsewhere. Subsequent media coverage has highlighted many of the themes discussed here; prominent examples include Susie Cagle, "The environmentalist roots of anti-immigrant bigotry" *The Guardian* August 16, 2019, and Joel Achenbach, "Two mass murders a world apart share a common theme: 'Ecofascism'" *Washington Post* August 18, 2019.

35 For insightful treatments of North American trends see Noel Sturgeon, *Environmentalism in Popular Culture: Gender, Race, Sexuality, and the Politics of the Natural* (Tucson: University of Arizona Press, 2009); Sarah Ray, *The Ecological Other:*

Environmental Exclusion in American Culture (Tucson: University of Arizona Press, 2013); Dorceta Taylor, *The Rise of the American Conservation Movement: Power, Privilege, and Environmental Protection* (Durham: Duke University Press, 2016). In US contexts, political assessment of the history of environmental movements is complicated by the anti-statist currents in right-wing thought. This factor has made it more difficult to recognize "the conservative roots of modern environmentalism." (William Cronon, "Conservative Conservationists," Foreword to Brian Drake, *Loving Nature, Fearing the State: Environmentalism and Antigovernment Politics before Reagan*, Seattle: University of Washington Press, 2013, xiii.) For critical discussion of such tendencies in the far right milieu see the chapter on "Decentralism" in Matthew Lyons, *Insurgent Supremacists: The U.S. Far Right's Challenge to State and Empire* (Oakland: PM Press, 2018), 144-60.

36 Carolyn Merchant, *Reinventing Eden: The Fate of Nature in Western Culture* (New York: Routledge, 2013), 206.

2.

A Revolution Against Technology

The Unabomber Manifesto
in Historical Context

> Over the years we have given as much attention to the development of our ideas as to the development of bombs, and we now have something serious to say. And we feel that just now the time is ripe for the presentation of anti-industrial ideas.
>
> — Unabomber communiqué to *New York Times* April 20, 1995

From 1978 until 1995, over the course of seventeen years, twenty-three people were injured and three killed in bombing attacks attributed to the "Unabomber." Calling himself an anarchist and preaching a "revolution against technology," the Unabomber appeared to be a madman with a mission. His targets included scientists, technicians, academics, computer professionals, airline employees, and advertising executives.[1] According to Ted Kaczynski, the former mathematics professor eventually convicted of these crimes, the point of the lengthy campaign of destruction was a quixotic quest to overthrow "industrial society." Seven months before Kaczynski was arrested at his remote Montana cabin, a voluminous document entitled "Industrial Society and Its Future" was published in mainstream newspapers across the United States.[2] The circumstances of its publication were as peculiar as its content.

The 35,000 word jeremiad that immediately became known as the "Unabomber Manifesto" appeared as a special eight-page supplement jointly published by the *New York Times* and the *Washington Post* on September 19, 1995. It was subsequently republished in a variety of other news outlets before taking on a life of its own on the internet. Kaczynski had been in anonymous contact with the New York Times since June 1993, and throughout 1995 negotiated with the newspaper about publication of the Manifesto. In an April 1995 letter to the *Times* Kaczynski wrote:

> Through our bombings we hope to promote social instability in industrial society, propagate anti-industrial ideas and give encouragement to those who hate the industrial system. [...] The people who are pushing all this growth and progress garbage deserve to be severely punished. But our goal is less to punish them than to propagate ideas. Anyhow we are getting tired of making bombs. It's no fun to have to spend all your evenings and weekends preparing dangerous mixtures, filing trigger mechanisms out of scraps of metal or searching the

sierras for a place isolated enough to test a bomb. So we offer
a bargain.[3]

If the Manifesto was published, the anonymous author assured his interlocutors, "we will permanently desist from terrorist activities." In the wake of a protracted series of bombings that had left many victims but few leads, this quid pro quo seemed to offer a break in the case. On the advice of federal investigators, the *Times* agreed to the deal.[4] The original manuscript of the Manifesto arrived at the newspaper on June 28, 1995, as a sixty-two page single-spaced document divided into 232 numbered paragraphs with thirty-six additional endnotes. Thus was "Industrial Society and Its Future" brought to the attention of the public. Kaczynski's hope evidently was that the master's tools might be used to dismantle the master's house.[5]

An anti-industrial gospel disseminated via the mass media, joined to an anti-technological praxis centered on intricately engineered explosive devices delivered through the postal service, may seem hopelessly incoherent. Despite such ironies, however, the Unabomber Manifesto merits close attention as a distinctively modern missive on redemption via destruction. It offers a narrative of technology and its discontents, of transgression and transcendence. In its pages Kaczynski paints an apocalyptic portrait of industrial society as a barren arena of total technical control with no room for human freedom or wild nature. Escaping this nightmare, we are told, and redeeming humanity and the natural world, will require the complete repudiation of technology as such.

Making sense of this notorious text and its improbable context presents a number of interpretive challenges and engages a wide range of debates in history, philosophy, and social criticism. I will address some of the more pertinent ones here, particularly those that have been neglected in previous discussions of the Manifesto and its antecedents. My argument will concentrate on three levels of analysis: the message of the Manifesto itself; its resonance with contemporary discourses on nature, freedom, and violence; and the specific ideological lineage within which "Industrial Society and Its Future" can best be understood. For although the Manifesto is in many respects a quintessentially American text, it echoes in sometimes uncanny ways a series of European reflections on the perils of technological progress.[6]

Against those interpreters of the Unabomber phenomenon who view its rejection of technology (whether approvingly or disapprovingly) as an extension of left critiques of untrammeled corporate industrialism, I present an alternative context within which to examine Kaczynski's pronouncements: the tradition of right-wing skepticism toward technology developed by German thinkers in the first half of the twentieth century. Since this tradition is not well known, I will devote considerable space to exposition of these ideas and trace their parallels within the Manifesto itself. Conceptual continuities of this sort reveal hitherto unnoticed aspects of the Manifesto's argument and its public reception.

Along with their roots in the right, I will examine the specific connections between Kaczynski's beliefs and those of various anarchists and radical political ecologists who have staked out a variety of positions on similar issues, some of which converge with the program outlined in the Manifesto while others contest its basic assumptions. My task here goes beyond reconstruction of past and present intellectual trends toward a critical engagement with these ongoing debates. I will argue that scholars, social thinkers, and activists alike would do well to take the Unabomber Manifesto seriously as a powerful form of protest grounded in genuine concerns, while subjecting its core claims to careful analysis. This is more than a historical exercise; the project Kaczynski publicized still inspires eager emulation today.

Though the focus here will be on philosophical precursors to the Manifesto, its possible literary influences are noteworthy as well. Perhaps the most obvious of these is Joseph Conrad's novel *The Secret Agent*, with its themes of anarchism, terrorist bombing, anti-science sentiment, and a professor gone over to violent extremism.[7] Dostoevsky is a further possibility, along with Karel Capek, Aldous Huxley, and Yevgeni Zamyatin.[8] This list could be extended to Goethe's Faust and Shelley's Frankenstein, to Thoreau and the Romantics and beyond, yet we have little direct information about what Kaczynski may have read, hence such hypotheses remain speculative.[9]

The usual genealogy of these ideas traces back to Rousseau, but there is a remarkable precursor in Shakespeare. Gonzalo's soliloquy in Act II of *The Tempest* reads:

> In the commonwealth I would by contraries
> Execute all things; for no kind of traffic
> Would I admit; no name of magistrate;

Letters should not be known; riches, poverty,
And use of service, none; contract, succession,
Bourn, bound of land, tilth, vineyard, none;
No use of metal, corn, or wine, or oil;
No occupation; all men idle, all;
And women too, but innocent and pure;
No sovereignty; — [...]

All things in common nature should produce
Without sweat or endeavour: treason, felony,
Sword, pike, knife, gun, or need of any engine,
Would I not have; but nature should bring forth,
Of its own kind, all foison, all abundance,
To feed my innocent people. [...]

I would with such perfection govern, sir,
To excel the golden age.[10]

This Arcadian vision, with its echoes of Montaigne, continues to animate a wide array of anti-industrial visionaries.[11] These anarchists, primitivists, and critics of technological myopia are Kaczynski's closest contemporaries, and the broader body of work they represent lends a measure of coherence to the Manifesto's occasionally inscrutable claims. Because such dissident perspectives deserve a more thorough hearing than they typically receive, the public attention given to the Unabomber's beliefs offers an important opportunity to re-assess radical critiques of technology. But this ideological terrain can be treacherous to navigate; those who traverse it frequently veer right and left in erratic ways, politically disoriented and heedless of the historical reverberations of the arguments they advance.[12] In this light, our task is to decipher the implications of Kaczynski's doctrines and examine their intellectual roots.

Since its publication, many commentators have dismissed the Unabomber Manifesto as mere nihilism[13] while others have seen it as an extension of radical left criticisms of contemporary society.[14] Both readings are wide of the mark. Whatever one makes of his bloody methods and his callous attitude toward his victims, the Unabomber's message is emphatically not an expression of nihilism, but a forceful statement of articulated ideals. The content of the Manifesto might well be considered a distorted form of utopianism, the opposite of nihilism.[15] More consequential is the erroneous correlation with the left. Although both defenders and critics of the Manifesto assigned it to the left end of the spectrum of critiques of overweening technology, the principal thrust of "Industrial Society and Its Future" belongs firmly to the right. Kaczynski rehearses a common version of right-wing discourse on the abuses of technological civilization, coupled with an atomistic conception of human liberty and a naïve understanding of nature.

This political perspective takes a variety of forms, some of them not immediately recognizable. Kaczynski's analysis aligns the Manifesto with the individualist strands within anarchism and the biocentric strands within ecological politics. It displays consistent parallels to the legacy of anti-industrial and proto-ecological thinking on the German right, an often overlooked but influential body of thought.[16] Even more perceptive and historically informed interpreters of the Manifesto, while offering insightful readings on several points, miss its most significant tropes and most revealing contexts, and thereby misunderstand the trajectory of the Manifesto as a whole.[17] Kaczynski is above all a critic of decadence and a prophet of regeneration through violence. The tradition he invokes is that of right-wing *Kulturkritik* and *Zivilisationskritik*, the reactionary critique of civilization as such.[18] To draw out these conceptual parallels, a detailed examination of the Manifesto is in order.*

"Industrial Society and Its Future" states its argument in stark terms as a primordial "conflict of technology vs. nature" (188, 191) and repeatedly declares "destruction" as its goal (135, 166, 200, 222). The Manifesto begins by claiming, understandably enough, that "industrial society" has "inflicted severe damage on the natural world."[19] Kaczynski warns that "continued development of technology" will "inflict greater damage on the natural world" (1). The basic parameters are established at the outset: the mere existence of technology, of whatever sort, is a threat to nature, and consequently technology itself must be destroyed.[20] "We

---

* I will quote from the first book edition: *The Unabomber Manifesto: Industrial Society and Its Future* (Berkeley: Jolly Roger Press, 1995), which apart from minor typographic discrepancies is identical to the original September 19, 1995 version. Due to the large number of subsequently published online and print editions, I will cite paragraph numbers rather than page numbers, as well as the separately numbered "Notes" that Kaczynski appended to the main text. All ellipses are mine; all emphases in original; I have changed the mode of emphasis from ALL CAPITALS to *italics*.

therefore advocate a revolution against the industrial system." (4) Throughout the Manifesto, "the industrial system" and "technology" are the culprits, without modifiers, qualification, or specification; it is "technology" per se that stands accused.[21] For Kaczynski, "the isolation of man from nature" is a straightforward result of "technological progress." (48) Hence of "the industrial system" he says quite simply: "we must destroy it." (135) Anything less than destruction is futile, for if "the development of technology" continues, it will "advance toward its logical conclusion, which is complete control over everything on Earth" (163).[22] The task that Kaczynski sets himself is nothing less than "to overthrow the whole technological system" (141).

But "wild nature" (5) is not the only victim of unrestrained technological advance. Kaczynski is equally concerned with the dire effects on human freedom. The heart of "the system" is "control over people and nature" (164). This conjunction of freedom and nature is one of the more promising strands within the Manifesto, indicating potential affiliations with radical proposals in ecological ethics and nature philosophy as well as contemporary anarchist thought. But the specific analysis of human freedom that Kaczynski advances is crucial to the argument of the Manifesto as a whole, and clearly distinguishes its approach from the emancipatory alternatives put forward by other anarchists and ecological thinkers. In continued reliance on the amorphous category of "technology," Kaczynski writes that his goal is "to protect freedom from technology" (111, repeated verbatim 136). Negative effects on human freedom are simply "the fault of technology" (119). This conspicuously decontextualized diagnosis is accompanied by a conservative conception of freedom as unimpeded liberty.

The Manifesto complains that "modern man is strapped down by a network of rules and regulations (explicit or implicit) that frustrate many of his impulses," ascribing this presumably dismal state of affairs to "industrial society." (71) It is an ahistorical and psychologically naïve argument; nowhere is the possibility acknowledged that the regulation of some impulses may be a fundamental aspect of every society, indeed of sociality as such.[23] Kaczynski instead remains committed to a definition of "freedom" as pursuit of individual goals "without interference, manipulation or supervision from anyone" (94). He even looks askance at "traffic regulations" as an impingement on freedom (127).[24] At the same time, the Manifesto sharply distinguishes between "freedom" and "permissiveness" (72, 94), condemning the latter, and dismisses religious freedom and sexual freedom as "unimportant." (72)

In contrast to the illegitimate constraints of technological society and the illicit permissiveness of modernity, Kaczynski promotes the ostensible virtues of self-sufficiency via an idealized image of the nineteenth century American frontier and the lifeways of "primitive" peoples.[25] Preaching the virtues of rugged individualism and self-reliance against the chronic dependency of the modern era (67-68), he appeals to the robust character of "the 19th-century frontiersman" in opposition to "modern man" (57). He similarly invokes "primitive man" (71) as counterpole to the debilitating effects of modern life. The Manifesto declares that "primitive peoples" are often "quite content to sit for hours at a time doing nothing at all, because they are at peace with themselves and their world. But most modern people must be constantly occupied or entertained, otherwise they get 'bored,' i.e. they get fidgety, uneasy, irritable." (147) This is a classic combination of laudable ideals – people at peace with themselves and their world – and suspect conjectures about the lifeways of both "primitive peoples" and "modern people," linked via the standard trope of posing the former as foil for the latter.[26] Each of these arguments depends on problematic assumptions about historical and anthropological difference, and their combined effect is to obscure the normative bases for Kaczynski's critique of contemporary society.

Those premises, once unearthed, are eminently questionable. Kaczynski fears the "decadent" and admires "fighting aristocracies" (34). He warns against "sinking into decadent hedonism" (38). His analysis is suffused with a longing for the rigor and discipline of a society based on hard work and genuine needs (41), the antithesis of distraction and dissolution; a world of hardened individuals pursuing authentic goals.[27] His chief complaint about life in modern society is that it is not demanding enough (e.g. 59-64 and Notes 10 and 12). He yearns for "a stable framework" and "a sense of security" (49), as well as a return to "traditional values." (50)

The Manifesto's litany of the ill effects of modern life is remarkably profuse; it includes not only "anxiety," "boredom," and "eating disorders" but also "child abuse, insatiable hedonism, abnormal sexual behavior" and "sexual perversion" (44) as alarming symptoms of the cultural-psychological decline induced by industrial society. Its debauched character results in "communities that are emasculated, tamed and made into tools of the system." (52) Such a society is a departure from "the natural pattern of human behavior" and contradicts "natural human impulses." (115)[28]

In light of these invidious assumptions, it is scarcely surprising to find Kaczynski fulminating against the left. Denunciations of "leftism" constitute the bulk of the Manifesto; there is some reference to it in nearly a third of the paragraphs, scattered throughout the document, and it is the central theme of both the first and the last titled sections ("The Psychology of Modern Leftism" and "The Danger of Leftism" respectively), the latter the second-longest section of the text overall. Kaczynski characterizes "leftism" as a specific kind of psychopathology, offering extended descriptions of what the category refers to: "the spectrum of related creeds that includes the feminist, gay rights, political correctness, etc., movements" (218). He continues:

"When we speak of leftists in this article we have in mind mainly socialists, collectivists, 'politically correct' types, feminists, gay and disability activists, animal rights activists and the like." (7) Leftists support "gun control," "sex education," "affirmative action" and "multiculturalism" (229); their ranks include "minority rights activists" (11); they use "the common catch-phrases of the left like 'racism,' 'sexism,' 'homophobia,' 'capitalism,' 'imperialism,' 'neocolonialism,' 'genocide,' 'social change,' 'social justice,' 'social responsibility.'" (229) Kaczynski reserves a special animosity for feminism. Paragraph 14 reads in its entirety: "Feminists are desperately anxious to prove that women are as strong and as capable as men. Clearly they are nagged by a fear that women may *not* be as strong and as capable as men."

Kaczynski categorically rejects any compromise with the left as he defines it, and insists on rigorously excluding left elements from the revolution against industrialism. He is unequivocal on this point: "a movement that exalts nature and opposes technology must take a resolutely anti-leftist stance and must avoid all collaboration with leftists." (214) The Manifesto points out that "radical environmentalism" includes both leftists and non-leftists, and excoriates those radical environmentalists "who ought to know better than to collaborate with leftists." (227) According to this analysis, "The leftist is anti-individualistic, pro-collectivist" (16) and has "a negative attitude toward individualism." (229) Leftism is "inconsistent with wild nature" and with "human freedom" because it is "collectivist" and believes in "organized society" (214). If leftists ever get technology "under their own control," they will "use it to oppress everyone else" (216). Kaczynski dismisses "social justice" as a goal; petty concerns about economic deprivation and disparity, about adequate food and clothing, "must not be allowed to interfere with the effort to get rid of the technological system." (201) Ethnic exclusion and racial justice are similarly "superficial matters" (29) and merely "of peripheral significance." (192)

Much of Kaczynski's polemic against the left reads like a parody of right-wing prejudices: "Leftists tend to hate anything that has an image of being strong, good and successful. They hate America, they hate Western civilization, they hate white males, they hate rationality." (15) Indeed, "Self-hatred is a leftist trait." (20) But this is no parody, and the sour note of anti-left ressentiment resounds throughout the Manifesto. Long stretches of the screed against "leftism" are nevertheless virtually irrelevant to its broader argument, consisting largely of an amalgam of pop sociobiology and irritation about the alleged excesses of "political correctness" in the academy, mixed with antagonism toward affirmative action and initiatives for gender equity. At times Kaczynski sounds like a critic of degenerate art: "Art forms that appeal to modern leftist intellectuals tend to focus on sordidness, defeat and despair, or else they take an orgiastic tone" (17). He does on occasion offer perfunctory criticism of "some conservatives" (Note 30), namely those who "enthusiastically support technological progress and economic growth." (50)[29] But these passing remarks seem insignificant in light of his unqualified condemnation of "leftism" as a whole.

Central as these arguments are to Kaczynski's case against modern society, the Manifesto is not exhausted by wholesale repudiation of technology, cultural decay, and the sins of the left. Kaczynski also has a positive alternative to offer. In place of the sterility and corruption of science, technology, and industrial organization, he holds out the promise of an utterly different world. This vision is founded on the idea of "wild nature."[30] In the words of the Manifesto: "The positive ideal that we propose is Nature. That is, *wild* nature; those aspects of the functioning of the Earth and its living things that are independent of human management and free of human interference and control." (183) Proclaiming that "nature is beautiful," Kaczynski expounds "an ideology that exalts nature and opposes technology." (184) This ideology will not only be beneficial to the natural world but to its human inhabitants as well: "Whatever kind of society may exist after the demise of the industrial system, it is certain that most people will live close to nature." (184)

The Manifesto provides a number of reasons for adopting an ideology of wild nature. "Nature makes a perfect counter-ideal to technology for several reasons. Nature (that which is outside the power of the system) is the opposite of technology (which seeks to expand indefinitely the power of the system)." (184) Kaczynski evokes the religious character of this ideology as well. Noting that "there is a religious vacuum in our society that could perhaps be filled by a religion focused on nature in opposition to technology," he writes: "A further advantage of nature as a counter-ideal to technology is that, in many people, nature inspires the kind of reverence that is associated with religion, so that nature could perhaps be idealized on a religious basis. [...] Thus it may be useful to introduce a religious element into the rebellion against technology, the more so because Western society today has no strong religious foundation." (Note 30)

With its enemies clearly identified and its alternative vision at hand, the Manifesto dauntlessly draws the consequences. Along with a massive "reduction of the population" (167), a "breakdown of technological civilization itself" (133) will be necessary for the redemption of humanity and the planet. Kaczynski insists that "the system cannot be reformed in such a way as to reconcile freedom with technology. The only way out is to dispense with the industrial-technological system altogether." (140) Overthrowing it will require "a revolution against the industrial-technological system." (141) The revolutionaries must be committed "exclusively to the destruction of technology." (222) Kaczynski's revolution adamantly prohibits all other aims; he reiterates that revolutionary energies must be mobilized "for only *one* purpose: to attack the technological system." (202) Since "the single overriding goal must be the elimination of modern technology" (206), he insists, "Until the industrial system has been thoroughly wrecked, the destruction of that system must be the revolutionaries' *only* goal." (200)

To reach this goal Kaczynski argues for a strategy of tension, deliberately intensifying social instability in order to hasten complete technological collapse. He recognizes that "If the system breaks down there may be a period of chaos," which will give those who survive "a new chance." (165) Hence the "revolution against technology" must take a two-pronged approach: "the two main tasks for the present are to promote social stress and instability in industrial society and to develop and propagate an ideology that opposes technology and the industrial system." (181) The Manifesto spells out what this strategy will entail:

> Therefore two tasks confront those who hate the servitude to which the industrial system is reducing the human race. First, we must work to heighten the social stresses within the system so as to increase the likelihood that it will break down or be weakened sufficiently so that a revolution against it becomes possible. Second, it is necessary to develop and propagate an ideology that opposes technology and the industrial society if and when the system becomes sufficiently weakened. And such an ideology will help to assure that, if and when industrial society breaks down, its remnants will be smashed beyond repair, so that the system cannot be reconstituted. The factories should be destroyed, technical books burned, etc. (166)

These methods and their bleak consequences are consistent with Kaczynski's own practice, bombs combined with doctrines. "Industrial Society and Its Future," in the manner of its delivery and publication, is an instantiation of its own logic. For the Unabomber, the medium is the message: "In order to get our message before the public with some chance of making a lasting impression, we've had to kill people." (96)

Though Kaczynski's work betrays little awareness of it, there is a lengthy tradition of political violence in the name of transcendent goals. Within the broad spectrum of anarchist thought, perhaps the most influential justification is Georges Sorel's 1908 treatise *Reflections on Violence*.[31] Equally relevant, in view of Kaczynski's reliance on "nature" and the quasi-messianic tone of the Manifesto, is Walter Benjamin's 1921 essay in response to Sorel, "Critique of Violence."[32] There are undoubtedly echoes in the Unabomber Manifesto of Sorel's conception of violence as redemptive; the Manifesto's propagation of an all-encompassing ideology that opposes technology and exalts nature might even be seen as a variation on Sorel's notion of "myth" as a counterforce to prevailing societal assumptions. In crucial respects, however, Kaczynski's proposed strategy and actual practice represent a return to an earlier phase of anarchist uses of violence, the late nineteenth century era of propaganda of the deed. This tactic focused on assassinating politicians, aristocrats, and industrialists, often by bombings. Such attacks proved ineffective as a catalyst to revolution, and the anarchist movement largely abandoned propaganda of the deed by the 1920s.[33] The Unabomber phenomenon is a revival of that older and seemingly discredited legacy.

A related question concerns the particular strands within the anarchist tradition that bear the strongest resemblance to Kaczynski's approach. His very first letter to the media began with the words: "We are an anarchist group calling ourselves FC." A later communiqué repeated: "We call ourselves anarchists."[34] As the Manifesto itself points out, however, Kaczynski espoused a "particular brand of anarchism." (Note 34) His brand is notably individualistic, affiliated with a tendency in anarchist thought that extends back to Max Stirner. This strand of anarchism has long been at odds with the communal tendencies in anarchist practice over the last century and a half that are sometimes grouped under the rubric of social anarchism. From a social anarchist perspective, the "particular brand of anarchism" championed by Kaczynski incorporates some of the most dubious elements of the tradition as a whole.[35]

Such intra-anarchist debates do not focus solely on individualism; they include several other themes that are central to the Unabomber Manifesto as well. The two most immediately relevant are the dispute over left-wing and right-wing influences within anarchism, and the contentious question of primitivism. Of those contemporary anarchists who find the Manifesto's message appealing, most are unsurprisingly hostile to the left as such.[36] Many of them identify strongly with the individualist tradition. While denying any special attachment to the right, they focus on furious denunciations of the left, sometimes proclaiming themselves "neither left nor right."[37] A number of these anarchists have proven receptive to the Manifesto's arguments.[38]

The primitivist strand of contemporary anarchism provided an even more congenial home for Kaczynski's ideas.[39] Centered on an array of periodicals devoted to "the destruction of civilization," this tendency's most influential spokesperson is John Zerzan.[40] Zerzan defended the Unabomber Manifesto from the moment it appeared, and he and Kaczynski conducted an extensive correspondence after the latter's arrest.[41] Much of Zerzan's work revolves around a critique of domestication, analogizing humans under industrial conditions with domestic animals, while proclaiming a re-assertion of wildness as alternative, to be achieved through a total "refusal of technology."[42] With an eclectic philosophical background, Zerzan was for a time a more articulate advocate of Kaczynski's views, preaching the imminent collapse of industrial civilization and an absolutist anti-technological stance. An apocalyptic sense of impending catastrophe pervades his work, linked to a millenarian vision of redemption through destruction focused on technological doom and undomesticated rebirth.[43]

These particular wings of contemporary anarchism appear to have exercised an important influence on Kaczynski's thinking while he was still at large. In his April 1995 message to the *New York Times* he wrote: "anyone who will read the anarchist and radical environmentalist journals will see that opposition to the industrial-technological system is widespread and growing."[44] Kaczynski himself contributed to all three of these strands within latter-day anarchist discourse, pursuing an individualist argument, an anti-left argument, and a primitivist argument in his writings both before and after the Unabomber Manifesto.[45]

Kaczynski developed these ideas across a span of decades. A 1971 anti-tech essay that he distributed among friends and family members, a sort of ur-text of the later Manifesto, begins as follows: "In these pages it is argued that continued scientific and technical progress will inevitably result in the extinction of individual liberty."[46] The final page of the essay bemoans "the ceaseless extension of society's power." Thirty years later, in a 2001 letter to *Green Anarchy*, Kaczynski continued the line of reasoning on "leftism" that he expounded at length in the Manifesto, reproaching the Zapatistas in Chiapas for not seeking "an end to modernity."[47] Declaring such endeavors typical of the left, he denounced the Zapatistas for trying to bring electricity, plumbing, and medicine to indigenous communities in southern Mexico.

In 2002 Kaczynski offered an updated version of the Unabomber Manifesto's core arguments, under the title "Hit Where It Hurts."[48] Addressed as a rallying cry to "opponents of the techno-industrial system," the article calls for a fundamental challenge to "the system."[49] Carefully avoiding any exhortations to illegal action, Kaczynski reminds his readers that "technology is the target" and that for the sake of "wilderness" a "life-and-death struggle" will be necessary. He flatly rejects pragmatic options such as "developing cleaner methods of generating electricity." Ecologically sustainable technology is still technology. "To accomplish anything against the system you have to attack all electric-power generation as a matter of principle, on the ground that dependence on electricity makes people dependent on the system."[50] Finally, Kaczynski recommends biotechnology as the most promising target for concerted attack.[51] Arguing that biotechnology is "central to the whole enterprise of technological progress," he focuses on "research scientists" and "corporate executives" as the lynchpin of the industry, and maintains that "persuading" these figures to "get out of biotech" would be the best way "to hit the system where it really hurts."[52]

Taking the totality of these texts into account, with the Unabomber Manifesto at their center, the outlines of Kaczynski's argument come into sharper relief. "Industrial Society and Its Future" presents a classic example of a familiar but often misunderstood genre: a fierce indictment of modern artificiality in the name of an imagined authenticity. Among twentieth-century critics of untrammeled technological advance, two figures are frequently invoked as possible influences on the Manifesto: Lewis Mumford and Jacques Ellul.[53] Both are reasonable choices; Mumford was arguably the most influential voice along these lines in an American context in the post-war period, and Kaczynski himself cited Ellul.

There are, however, significant differences between these critics of technological complacency and Kaczynski's totalizing renunciation of technology in all its forms. While Mumford discussed "organization man" and the role of "control" in terms similar to the Manifesto, his approach displayed a powerful sense of the aesthetic dimension of technological artifacts and stressed the mutual interplay of technology and culture. In his earlier work he rejected technological determinism and maintained a basically optimistic view of the possibilities for a humanized and ecologized technics.[54] Mumford's writings on urbanism are also at odds with the anti-urban sentiments of latter-day primitivists. Even Mumford's later work *The Myth of the Machine*, whose argument is closer to that of

Kaczynski, Zerzan, et al., concludes on a note of possibility and renewal rather than evoking a technological Ragnarok.[55] In Mumford's own words, his work is "far from disparaging the role of technics."[56] He held that it was a particular cultural matrix and a constellation of specific social structures that led to the rise of what he called the "megamachine."[57]

Ellul's analysis is in some respects more compatible with Kaczynski's. The French philosopher and theologian was a technological determinist regarding modern technical apparatuses, and he described the "automatic growth" of technology as "a self-generating process."[58] But unlike his anti-civilization acolytes, Ellul held a positive view of civilization and its capacity for moderating technological structures and imperatives. He praised ancient Greek society, with its judicious self-chosen limits on technological forms, as "an apex of civilization" and was confident that in other historical contexts a humanist ethos had served to restrain technological growth.[59] Unlike previous eras, however, Ellul believed that by the twentieth century the threshold had been crossed: "Today technique has taken over the whole of civilization." Thus in our time technology "desacralizes men and things," and the technological system "eliminates or subordinates the natural world."[60]

These arguments are a clear precursor to the Manifesto. Ellul characterized the present situation as "all or nothing," declaring: "If we make use of technique, we must accept the specificity and autonomy of its ends, and the totality of its rules. Our own desires and aspirations can change nothing."[61] In a later work, on the other hand, Ellul wrote: "the issue is not technology *per se*, but the present structure of society."[62] Ellul was sympathetic to anarchism, from his eclectic Christian viewpoint, but emphatically repudiated violent acts: "By anarchy I mean first an absolute rejection of violence. Hence I cannot accept either nihilists or anarchists who choose violence as a means of action."[63] Ellul's thought thus yields a mixed legacy in regard to Kaczynski's program of violent upheaval against technology.

Other possible influences have been proposed in addition to Mumford and Ellul. Tim Luke, for example, contends that the Unabomber Manifesto "parallels Marcuse's reading of technology."[64] Although several terminological correspondences may be noted between the Manifesto's vocabulary and Marcuse's writings, this interpretation is untenable. Marcuse disagreed with Kaczynski on virtually every substantive issue, from nature to political violence to hedonism to technology to freedom to the structure of psychological drives and the "origins of the repressed individual."[65] Even *One-Dimensional Man*, Marcuse's bleakest work and the closest in tone to the Manifesto, forcefully contradicts Kaczynski on several crucial points. In these pages Marcuse does indeed write:

> Technological rationality reveals its political character as it becomes the great vehicle of better domination, creating a truly totalitarian universe in which society and nature, mind and body are kept in a state of permanent mobilization for the defense of this universe.[66]

But the very emphasis on the "political character" of technological rationality is at odds with Kaczynski's approach, which thoroughly discounts "political structure" (Note 33) and repeatedly rejects "political revolution" (4, 193). Marcuse, in contrast, held that "the techniques of industrialization are political techniques" and insisted on the possibility of a different form of technology: "The technological transformation is at the same time political transformation, but the political change would turn into qualitative social change only to the degree to which it would alter the direction of technical progress— that is, develop a new technology."[67] Marcuse held open the potential for "science and technology" to "pass beyond" their current form and lead toward an overcoming of oppression. He argued that "technological rationality, freed from its exploitative features," could become part of a liberated and self-directing society at peace with its natural surroundings.[68]

The origins of Kaczynski's conception of technology and society are not to be found in the work of left theorists like Marcuse.[69] As contemporary anarcho-primitivist fans of the Unabomber Manifesto have come to recognize, some of their true predecessors are thinkers of the German right who took a skeptical view of technology and industrialism. Although there is little mention of such figures in the existing literature on the Manifesto, it is to right-wing theorists like Ludwig Klages, Oswald Spengler, and Friedrich Georg Jünger that we must look for consistent conceptual parallels to "Industrial Society and Its Future."[70] The affinities traced here are not a matter of direct ideological influence; there is little indication that Kaczynski was familiar with this literature.[71] Disregarded as they may be, these authors produced several of the most detailed critiques of modern technological life to emerge from the right in the twentieth century.

In a sense, Klages (1872-1956), Spengler (1880-1936), and Jünger (1898-1977) represent successive generations on the German right, with Klages a proponent of *Lebensphilosophie*, Jünger an advocate of the Conservative Revolution, and Spengler a mediating figure between the two currents.[72] Klages was a mystical philosopher who counterposed "biocentric" wisdom to the afflictions of rationalism and degeneration. Spengler gained notoriety for his sweeping chronicle of cultural devolution and grim prophecies about the fate of Western society. Jünger's ardent nationalism was matched by an unabashed elitism, the dual foundation for his vehement rejection of democracy. At a time when questions of technology, industry, and environmental decline were becoming pressing issues that generated little consensus on either the left or the right, these writers articulated a rightist response to increasing mechanization that was distinctively critical without simply calling for a return to plainer and purer times.[73]

Klages set the stage for this standpoint with his influential 1913 essay "Man and Earth." A favorite of the right wing of the ecology movement ever since, this seminal treatment begins by locating the source of the modern malaise in "science" and "technology."[74] The text continually identifies "progress" as a negative phenomenon while decrying the disappearance of wilderness and the expansion of industry. Klages bewails deforestation and the endangerment of animal species, proffering a catalogue of the deleterious effects of "progress" on people's lives, and warns against viewing the world as "a great machine."[75] He also makes reverential references to "the German landscape" and condemns capitalism,

Christianity, and science in one fell swoop.[76] These themes found continuation among a number of later figures on the German right.

Oswald Spengler's approach to the same constellation of topics was more complex. His major work on the subject, the 1931 book *Man and Technics*, was indebted to Klages in several respects.[77] To a greater extent than Klages, however, Spengler stressed technology's tendency to establish and impose its own logic, bringing his analysis an important step closer to Kaczynski's. *Man and Technics* is a brief but multifaceted text that stands in a somewhat ambiguous relationship to Spengler's famous earlier work *The Decline of the West*, and the later book on technology has received widely varying interpretations.[78]

Spengler posits an original state of human wildness as the exemplar of "perfect freedom" and opposes this primal self-sufficiency to the emasculating effects of ostensibly labor-saving technological devices, while simultaneously rebuking the "ever-increasing alienation from *all* Nature."[79] He characterizes technology as "unnatural" and holds it largely responsible for the "steadily increasing, fateful rift between man's world and the universe."[80] The book points to the emergence of agriculture and sedentary human communities as a fatal turning point; from then on, "the rolling stone is approaching the abyss in rapid leaps."[81] Spengler calls cities "*completely* anti-natural" and takes a decidedly dim view of "society" itself.[82] Directly prefiguring core themes in the Unabomber Manifesto, Spengler traces the decline "from *organic* to *organized* existence, from living in natural groups to living in artificial groupings," and laments the fact that the "creator *against* Nature," technological man, "has become the slave of his creation."[83] In mournful tones he declares:

> The mechanization of the world has entered on a phase of highly dangerous over-tension. [...] All things organic are dying in the grip of organization. An artificial world is permeating and poisoning the natural. Civilization itself has become a machine that does everything in mechanical fashion.[84]

Man and Technics goes on to invoke the "cold atmosphere of technical organization," and the book ends with a desolate vision of inevitable decline and eventual "catastrophe."[85] The affinities to "Industrial Society and Its Future" are pronounced. Like the Manifesto, Spengler invokes "unspoilt primitive people" as his positive contrast to the "modern technical process," while Kaczynski echoes Spengler in deploring the "isolation of man from nature, excessive rapidity of social change and the breakdown of natural small-scale communities" (47). Against the backdrop of the German right, the Unabomber Manifesto begins to appear in sharper political definition.

The final figure in this ideological sequence is Friedrich Georg Jünger, author of *The Failure of Technology*.[86] While not as well known as his older brother Ernst Jünger, Friedrich Georg Jünger was a prolific writer who played an important role in the circles of the non-Nazi right.[87] Unlike his brother, whose "heroic" treatments of technology from the 1920s and 1930s are renowned, Friedrich Georg Jünger adopted a skeptical stance toward technology from a relatively early stage.[88] *The Failure of Technology* criticizes "the entire technical organization."[89] Jünger rebuffs "all the illusions which technical progress creates" and maintains that technological progress is inextricably "coupled with a growth of organization, with a mushrooming bureaucracy."[90] His recurrent foes are "technology," "industry," "the machine," and "organization." For Jünger, "ruthless destruction of resources is the characteristic of our technology."[91] He denounces technology's impact on nature: "The machine invades the landscape with destruction and transformation [...] Technology darkens the air with smoke, poisons the water, destroys the plants and animals." The telos of technology is "the most complete and the most intensive exploitation on a planetary scale."[92]

Like Kaczynski, Jünger also attacks the degrading effects of technology on human life. The phrase "organization of the human" is repeated throughout the text as an anathema, and Jünger emphasizes that "technical progress and the formation of masses go hand in hand."[93] He deplores "the devastation of spiritual life which grows in step with mechanization."[94] *The Failure of Technology* identifies routinization and uniformity as the principal traits of a technology that has become self-perpetuating: "The autonomous, uniform, and repetitive function of mechanization is the chief characteristic of our technology."[95]

Jünger, Spengler, and Klages were not unique. Anguished forebodings about a looming technological deluge have been a regular refrain in German right-wing thought for many years. In his 1899 magnum opus *The Foundations of the Nineteenth Century*, a veritable reactionary bible better known for its celebration of Aryan superiority, Houston Stewart Chamberlain included a section titled "The

Machine" asserting that the devastation wrought by modern technology is "absolutely beyond conception." The rise of factories and an industrial workforce led him to regret the "inexpressible misery caused everywhere by the introduction of the machine," as evidenced by "the reduction of thousands and millions of human beings from relative prosperity and independence to continuous slavery, and their removal from the healthy life of the country to a miserable, light-less and airless existence in large cities."[96]

Half a century later, Martin Heidegger began his 1953 essay "The Question Concerning Technology" by noting: "Everywhere we remain unfree and chained to technology, whether we passionately affirm or deny it."[97] Apart from the competing tradition of left-wing critiques of industrialized capitalism and its technological configuration, there are other figures who do not fit neatly into the left-right spectrum and who developed profoundly critical accounts of technology and industrialism, such as Theodor Lessing or Günther Anders. Kaczynski and his epigones draw indiscriminately on this loose range of works and their popularized corollaries.[98] There are nevertheless too many distinctive continuities between the analysis proposed in the Unabomber Manifesto and the arguments put forward by Klages, Spengler and Jünger, and too many telltale signs in the text of the Manifesto, to ignore Kaczynski's debt to right-wing thought.[99] "Industrial Society and Its Future" assembles a collection of grievances common to multiple generations of reactionary theorists. This constellation of modern discontents is not in itself sufficient to locate Kaczynski's position within the tradition of right-wing *Kulturkritik* and

Zivilisationskritik, but when such complaints are framed by denunciations of decadence and dissipation, emasculation and perversion, and the pernicious role of leftism, the similarities are unmistakable.

These aspects of the Manifesto, in conjunction with the affinities to figures like Sorel and Evola, raise the specter of a possible proto-fascist reading of the Unabomber phenomenon. As scholars of fascism have noted, "The love of nature in fascist propaganda is a veiled reaction to failed civilization, a reactionary turn against the failure truly to liberate the human senses. [...] the lovers of nature are often also the most vicious killers."[100] Several complicating considerations should be taken into account: the specific strands of right-wing German thought canvassed here had an equivocal relationship to German varieties of fascism, National Socialist or otherwise; and aside from Nazism's deeply ambivalent stance on technics and nature, Italian Fascist attitudes toward ecological questions were not typically anti-technological.[101] Kaczynski's self-conception may perhaps be better understood as a species of the same "neither left nor right" thinking that animates several of the anarchist tendencies examined earlier and has found some resonance within ecological circles in recent decades. This desire to transcend the left-right continuum has a distinct historical pedigree tracing back to the early period of ideological consolidation within classical fascist and proto-fascist movements at the beginning of the last century.[102] Overall, the mixed historical record points to a generally rightist but not necessarily fascist milieu as the intellectual backdrop to many of the ideas Kaczynski promotes.

The fundamental shortcoming of the Unabomber Manifesto as a would-be call to revolution, however, is not that it consists of a rehash of right-wing shibboleths. Kaczynski's disquisition on the evils of modern technology fails as both critique and as reconstruction: neither its analyses nor its alternatives are adequate to the task of confronting a technological-industrial system gone awry. The Manifesto posits a conception of technology that is devoid of distinctions; not only is technology demonized, it is rendered monolithic. Kaczynski's undifferentiated hostility toward all things technological prevents him from taking seriously the crucial contrasts between divergent modes of technological practice.[103] This represents a significant departure from the original Luddite movement, whose target was not technology as such but the social relations expressed and enforced by a particular technological apparatus.[104]

Indeed the Manifesto seems to regard social relations as a mere epiphenomenon of technology; it is "technical advances" that have "created a world" deprived of freedom (128), rather than unfree social relations shaping a particular palette of technical choices. This stance erases the central insight on which other critiques of technological irrationality rest, namely that every technical artifact embodies social preferences, principles, and priorities, that every technological device represents and reinforces a specific set of social relationships. Kaczynski misconstrues this elemental reciprocity. He recognizes that "technology changes society" (127), but fails to consider the reverse, that societies also change the technologies they implement, that social factors frame the technological apparatus they produce and reproduce.[105] In his account, it is a static and one-way process in which technologies determine social relations, rather than a dynamic interaction between the two. Contrary to the Manifesto's one-dimensional framework, Langdon Winner writes:

> Different ideas of social and political life entail different technologies for their realization. One can create systems of production, energy, transportation, information handling, and so forth that are compatible with the growth of autonomous, self-determining individuals in a democratic polity.[106]

Against this socially mediated and technically nuanced view, "Industrial Society and Its Future" insists on the indivisibility of all technology: "The 'bad' parts of technology cannot be separated from the 'good' parts." (121) Like a golem unleashed, the technological juggernaut cannot be redirected or reconfigured, but only destroyed. For Kaczynski, "modern technology is a unified, tightly organized system, so that, in order to retain *some* technology, one finds oneself obliged to retain *most* technology" (200).[107] In his eyes, the process is both unilinear and irreversible: "technological progress marches in only one direction; it can never be reversed. [...] the system can move in only one direction, toward greater technologization." (129) The Manifesto explicitly rejects the idea of a "new kind of social order." (184) A "society that would reconcile freedom with technology" is simply impossible. (112)

Kaczynski's analysis forecloses the very possibility of technological innovations that are humane and ecologically sound.[108] He does not distinguish bicycles and windmills from nuclear power plants and internal combustion engines. For him, "technology" is simply an oppressive force without specific social contours, ubiquitous and uniform, an inevitably threatening impulse that presents human societies with a stark either-or choice: to accept it or reject it as a whole.[109] Even Kaczynski's concrete examples of techno-industrial perfidy display this superficial character. His article "Hit where it hurts" points to computers, electric power, and the communications sector, along with the entertainment industry, journalism, and advertising, as the heart of "the system"; Kaczynski says nothing about assembly lines, factory production, or Taylorist work regimens; there is no discussion of mining, no mention even of how computer chips are manufactured. His critique is entirely fixated on the shiny surface of technological gadgetry, not on the physical infrastructure that produces it, much less the social infrastructure that supports it. The myriad ways in which particular technologies incorporate and impose particular labor norms and particular usage patterns are foreign to his analysis. As a consequence, his writings do not register any sense of the social matrix of technological development.

In philosophical terms, the Unabomber Manifesto may be seen as a classic instance of abstract negation. The involuted entwinement of technological progress and social regress, however, calls for a much more finely calibrated determinate negation.[110] Nowhere is this more clear than in Kaczynski's image of wild nature as the alternative to technology run wild. Like Gonzalo's vision of a natural paradise, "innocent and pure," with "no use of metal" and no "need of any engine," Kaczynski conjures up "a nontechnological society" (Note

32) in a revived wilderness. The leitmotif of "wild nature" appears to have fueled much of Kaczynski's personal rage against the machine. In a journal entry from 1985 he wrote: "Have to get revenge for all the wild country being fucked up by the system."[111]

At the crux of the Manifesto's analysis lies a spurious conception of the natural world. This pivotal aspect of Kaczynski's philosophy places him close to the tradition of biocentric thinking, an approach better known in some quarters as deep ecology. Echoing Klages and others on the German right, Kaczynski himself has endorsed "the biocentric paradigm."[112] Identifying its adversary as "industrial society," the centerpiece of deep ecology's view of nature is the notion of wilderness, natural areas unaffected by human contact. In the biocentric worldview, humanity and nature form a fundamental dichotomy, and the task is to protect the latter from the former.[113] It is from this understanding of nature as the contrary of humanity, and of wild nature as a pristine realm untroubled by the presence of people, that the Manifesto's argument proceeds. But conceiving of nature in this way merely recapitulates the very division it seeks to overcome, and posits a purely imaginary alternative to a very real social and ecological crisis.[114] In one of the momentous ironies of the Manifesto, Kaczynski's perception of nature is ensnared within a decidedly modern and Euro-American paradigm.[115]

Against its own intentions, then, "Industrial Society and Its Future" emphatically demonstrates, in the words of Theodor Adorno, "how erroneous the crude antithesis of technology and nature is."[116] Adorno's diagnosis, composed before any of Kaczynski's bombs had been built, goes to the core of the Manifesto's failings and lays bare the social and ideological conditions out of which the Unabomber developed:

> Delight in nature was bound up with the conception of the subject as being-for-itself and virtually infinite in itself; as such the subject projected itself onto nature and in its isolation felt close to it; the subject's powerlessness in a society petrified into a second nature becomes the motor of the flight into a purportedly first nature. [...] In schema borrowed from bourgeois sexual morality, technology is said to have ravished nature, yet under transformed relations of production it would just as easily be able to assist nature and on this poor earth help it become what perhaps it would like to be.[117]

For Kaczynski, however, nature and freedom occupy an absolute status, one that sanctions violence as regenerative and salvific. In his longing to disrupt industrial society he has fashioned a false alternative, an ideology that claims to exalt nature and is announced by explosions. This ideology misunderstands both nature and freedom; the vision of redemption it proffers is poisoned at the root.[118] Kaczynski takes his place in an unlikely ideological lineage that encompasses proto-fascists and neo-primitivists. Eschewing the determinate negation of ecological despoliation and social misery in favor of a simpler scapegoat under the rubric of technology, the Unabomber Manifesto forgets its own historical context and political trajectory, in a hoped-for escape from a modernity gone mad.[119]

Though a product of its time, "Industrial Society and Its Future" continues to inspire admirers and adherents a quarter of a century after its appearance. With its frontier ethos and its myth of a manly hero standing up against overwhelming odds, the Unabomber story unwittingly replicates conventional expectations about the "masculine primitive" bravely resisting the "perils of civilization."[120] Kaczynski's beliefs have proven attractive to figures like Anders Breivik, who appropriated substantial portions of the Manifesto for his own crusade.[121] But the more significant contemporary influence emerges in various environmental offshoots seeking "the collapse of industrial civilization," from Derrick Jensen and "Deep Green Resistance" to Paul Kingsnorth's "Dark Ecology."[122] Today the Unabomber seems to be enjoying an online renaissance, drawing a new generation of enthusiasts.[123]

This resurgence of interest makes it all the more important to confront the flaws in Kaczynski's credo. If the future prophesied in the Manifesto remains a prisoner of its own unexamined past, what alternative outlook might there be? What could a different technological prospect look like? To those who are profoundly dissatisfied with the same ensemble of social and ecological conditions that Kaczynski so furiously denounces, a more dialectically complex approach to the topic is unlikely to provide the same kind of visceral identification. Yet the effort is vital nonetheless.

A critical perspective based on collective social transformation rather than catastrophism could be built around a contextual understanding of technology instead of a rigid technological determinism, reaching toward an integration of social and ecological values rather than hypostasizing their separation. This would mean actively re-shaping human engagement with technology instead of capitulating to the notion—apparently radical but essentially reactionary—that the very attempt to do so must have an inevitably warping effect. Such a critical perspective renounces the dream of regeneration through violence in order to overcome debasement. These are the sorts of conclusions that might have resulted from some of the Manifesto's reflections, but that in the end are impeded by the text itself, by the brutal conditions of its dissemination, and by its reception and interpretation so far.

Kaczynski's hope of transcending technological disaster in order to return to wild nature is a hollow ambition that mistakes its own origins and obstructs its own aims. Surmounting the current ecological crisis will mean more than simply changing or eliminating technical equipment; it will mean fundamentally reconstructing all of society from the ground up. Whether in local or global terms, as Chaia Heller observes, "There is no recipe for a 'good' or 'ecological' technology independent of a truly democratic context."[124] In Kaczynski's eyes, though, radical social transformation itself is inconsequential. That decisive error indicates how thoroughly ideologies of industrial apocalypse misunderstand the interrelationship between technology and its social underpinnings.[125] Devoid of this dialectical sensibility, Kaczynski is left with a grandiose but futile call for "a revolution against modernity, and against civilization in general."[126]

Viewed in its historical and philosophical setting, the revolution augured in the Unabomber Manifesto leads down dead-end paths. But its message is anything but moot. In reviving the half-forgotten arguments of reactionary theorists from the troubled Germany of the twentieth century, "Industrial Society and Its Future" has found a receptive audience among would-be radicals in the America of the twenty-first century. Its supposedly redemptive promise demands critical attention from thinkers and activists who wish to comprehend the history of our present technological predicament as well as the history of attempts to move beyond it.

Notes

1   The appellation "unabomber" reportedly referred to the
    prominence of universities and airlines among the early targets of
    the long-anonymous bomber. Details of the case can be found in
    popular treatments by Robert Graysmith, *Unabomber: A Desire
    to Kill* (Washington: Regnery, 1997) and Alston Chase, *Harvard
    and the Unabomber: The Education of an American Terrorist* (New
    York: Norton, 2003); both works are sensationalistic and should
    be consulted with care. An analysis of Kaczynski's trial is available
    in Michael Mello, *The United States of America versus Theodore
    John Kaczynski: Ethics, Power and the Invention of the Unabomber*
    (New York: Context, 1999).

2   Early versions of the Manifesto used the first person plural
    throughout, suggesting collective authorship, and were signed
    with the pseudonymous initials "FC." Now serving a life sentence
    in prison, Kaczynski has subsequently published the text under
    his own name; cf. Theodore Kaczynski, *The Road to Revolution:
    The Complete & Authorized Unabomber* (Oakville: Mosaic, 2009),
    19-100; Kaczynski, *Technological Slavery: The Collected Writings
    of Theodore J. Kaczynski, a.k.a. 'The Unabomber'* (Port Townsend;
    Feral House, 2010), 36-120. For the most recent statement of his
    views see Theodore Kaczynski, *Anti-Tech Revolution: Why and
    How* (Scottsdale: Fitch & Madison, 2020).

3   April 20, 1995 letter to New York Times, quoted in Graysmith,
    Unabomber, 298. This letter and other correspondence with the
    Times used a numeric code to establish authenticity of authorship.

4   The FBI's reasoning paid off when Kaczynski's estranged brother
    David read the published version of the Manifesto, recognized
    the writing style and content, and contacted the authorities. For

his memoir see David Kaczynski, *Every Last Tie: The Story of the Unabomber and His Family* (Durham: Duke University Press, 2016).

5   Compare Audre Lorde's critical reflection on the contradictions inherent in this approach to social transformation: Lorde, "The Master's Tools Will Never Dismantle the Master's House" in *Sister Outsider* (Trumansburg: Crossing Press, 1984), 110-13. A revealing historical survey of both bombs and print media as means to political ends can be found in Catherine Lavenir, "Bombs, Printers, and Pistols: A Mediological History of Terrorism" *History and Technology* vol. 19 no. 1 (2003), 54-62.

6   Alston Chase characterizes the Manifesto as "a compendium of philosophical and environmental clichés that expresses concerns shared by millions of Americans." Chase, *Harvard and the Unabomber*, 24. Many of Kaczynski's arguments about nature and technology stand within a specifically American tradition of thought; for contrasting accounts of this intellectual background see Leo Marx, *The Machine in the Garden: Technology and the Pastoral Ideal in America* (New York: Oxford University Press, 1964); Roderick Nash, *Wilderness and the American Mind* (New Haven: Yale University Press, 1967); David Nye, "Technology, Nature, and American Origin Stories" *Environmental History* vol. 8 no. 1 (2003), 8-24. Additional context is available in Arthur Melzer, ed., *Technology in the Western Political Tradition* (Ithaca: Cornell University Press, 1993); Mikel Hard, ed., *The Intellectual Appropriation of Technology: Discourses on Modernity, 1900-1939* (Cambridge: MIT Press, 1998); Daniel Headrick, *Power over Peoples: Technology, Environments, and Western Imperialism, 1400 to the Present* (Princeton: Princeton University Press, 2012).

7   Joseph Conrad, *The Secret Agent* (London: Methuen, 1907). The eerily prescient work of fiction may even have been the source

for the name "FC"; the anarchist group in the novel carries the moniker "FP" for "Future of the Proletariat." Kaczynski was reportedly a keen reader of Conrad, and a copy of *The Secret Agent* was found in his cabin in Montana after his arrest. On Kaczynski and Conrad see Don Foster, *Author Unknown* (New York: Holt, 2000), 15, 141. The third chapter of Foster's book offers a worthwhile analysis of Kaczynski's writing style and intellectual background. Another study of Kaczynski's rhetoric is available in the chapter on the Unabomber in Ian Hill, *Advocating Weapons, War, and Terrorism: Technological and Rhetorical Paradox* (University Park: Pennsylvania State University Press, 2018).

8   Karel Capek, *R.U.R.* (New York 1923); Aldous Huxley, *Brave New World* (London 1932); Yevgeni Zamyatin, *We* (New York 1952). Ernst Toller's 1922 play about the Luddites, *The Machine-Wreckers*, is another possibility.

9   Graysmith reports that "the FBI individually catalogued everything recovered from [Kaczynski's] cabin except the books"; his library included 233 volumes at the time of his arrest (Graysmith, *Unabomber*, 229). Partial lists of titles appear in Graysmith, *Unabomber*, 28, and Chase, *Harvard and the Unabomber*, 39. Access to this material has been complicated by federal court decisions ordering that items impounded from Kaczynski's cabin (including extensive unpublished writings) must be sold, with the proceeds going to compensate the Unabomber's victims; see "Unabomber's Papers Ordered to Be Sold" *New York Times* January 10, 2009, A14. On the post-1995 documents archived at the University of Michigan Library's Labadie Collection see Julie Herrada, "Letters to the Unabomber: A Case Study and Some Reflections" *Archival Issues* vol. 28, No. 1 (2004), 35-46.

10   William Shakespeare, *The Tempest* (New York: Penguin, 1999), 13.

11 Marx, *The Machine in the Garden*, 48-51 discusses the soliloquy
and notes its resonance with "primitivist-anarchist programs" (51).

12 Boris Frankel provides an astute guide to this territory in *The Post-Industrial Utopians* (Madison: University of Wisconsin Press, 1987).

13 Cf. Graysmith, *Unabomber*, 8 and Chase, *Harvard and the Unabomber*, 94 and 348.

14 This reading was shared by the mainstream *Newsweek* and
the left-leaning *Nation*; cf. Joe Klein, "The Unabomber and
the Left" *Newsweek* April 22, 1996, and Kirkpatrick Sale, "The
Unabomber's Secret Treatise: Is There Method in his Madness?"
The Nation September 25, 1995. For a conventional assessment
of the Manifesto as an inspiration for "environmental extremists"
see Brett Barnett, "20 Years Later: A Look Back at the Unabomber
Manifesto" *Perspectives on Terrorism* vol. 9 no. 6 (2015), 60-71.

15 On the psychoanalytic dimensions of this phenomenon see Joel
Whitebook, *Perversion and Utopia: A Study in Psychoanalysis and
Critical Theory* (Cambridge: MIT Press, 1995).

16 For overviews of this tradition compare Hermann Bausinger,
"Zwischen Grün und Braun" in Hubert Cancik, ed., *Religions-
und Geistesgeschichte der Weimarer Republik* (Düsseldorf:
Patmos, 1982), 215-29; Albrecht Lorenz and Ludwig Trepl,
"Grüne Schale – brauner Kern: Faschistische Strukturen
unter dem Deckmantel der Ökologie" *Politische Ökologie* 11
(1993), 17-24; Axel Goodbody, ed., *The Culture of German
Environmentalism: Anxieties, Visions, Realities* (Oxford: Berghahn,
2002); Friedemann Schmoll, "Vertraute und fremde Natur:
Zum Konnex ökologischer und völkischer Deutungsmuster"
in Hartmut Heller, ed., *Fremdheit im Prozess der Globalisierung*
(Berlin: Lit, 2007), 59-73. Despite distorted interpretations, useful
historical information can also be found in Rolf Peter Sieferle,

Fortschrittsfeinde: Opposition gegen Technik und Industrie von der Romantik bis zur Gegenwart (Munich: Beck, 1984) and Thomas Rohkrämer, *Eine andere Moderne? Zivilisationskritik, Natur und Technik in Deutschland 1880-1933* (Paderborn: Schöningh, 1999); both are the extended efforts to rehabilitate this tradition.

17 Compare Scott Corey, "On the Unabomber" *Telos* no. 118 (Winter 2000), 157-81, and Tim Luke, "Re-Reading the Unabomber Manifesto" *Telos* no. 107 (Spring 1996), 81-94; the latter appears in revised form in Luke, *Capitalism, Democracy, and Ecology* (Chicago: University of Illinois Press, 1999). Both Luke and Corey offer unduly sympathetic readings of the Manifesto, and neither successfully distinguishes right-wing variants of technophobic discourse from left-wing variants. This is perhaps not surprising in light of the political trajectory of *Telos* since the 1980s; on the curious convergence of right and left themes within this journal see Boris Frankel, "Confronting Neo-Liberal Regimes: The Post-Marxist Embrace of Populism and Realpolitik" *New Left Review* no. 226, December 1997; Tamir Bar-On, *Where have all the fascists gone?* (Aldershot: Ashgate, 2007), 149-64; Joseph Lowndes, "From New Class Critique to White Nationalism: *Telos*, the Alt Right, and the Origins of Trumpism" *Konturen* vol. 9 (2017), 8-12.

18 A distinctive feature of German right-wing thought for generations, the related traditions of *Kulturkritik* and *Zivilisationskritik* are difficult to convey in English; they sometimes referred to fears that the rise of "the machine" would destroy all organic bonds and leave a hollow shell in place of "natural" communal heritage. Fritz Ringer has described this ideology as a nebulous protest against "sterile, mechanical, and modern civilization." Ringer, *The Decline of the German Mandarins* (Cambridge: Harvard University Press, 1969), 259.

Another early critical analysis offers ample material about right-wing attacks on "industrial civilization": Fritz Stern, *The Politics of Cultural Despair: A Study in the Rise of the Germanic Ideology* (Berkeley: University of California Press, 1961), xi, xvi, xxvi, 60, 118, 122, 146. For further context compare Hans-Joachim Lieber, *Kulturkritik und Lebensphilosophie: Studien zur deutschen Philosophie der Jahrhundertwende* (Darmstadt: Wissenschaftliche Buchgesellschaft, 1974); Pier Paolo Portinaro, "Kulturpessimismus und die Grenzen der Entzauberung: Diagnosen zu Technik, Kultur und Politik nach der Jahrhundertwende" in Rüdiger vom Bruch, ed., *Kultur und Kulturwissenschaften um 1900: Krise der Moderne und Glaube an die Wissenschaft* (Stuttgart: Steiner, 1989), 175-96; Michael Spöttel, *Die ungeliebte 'Zivilisation': Zivilisationskritik und Ethnologie in Deutschland im 20. Jahrhundert* (Frankfurt: Lang, 1995); Georg Bollenbeck, *Eine Geschichte der Kulturkritik* (Munich: Beck, 2007). A lively history of left-wing *Kulturkritik* can also be found alongside the right-wing strand.

19   For a more historically specific account of the vague concept of industrial society see "The Rise of Industrial Society" in Ernst Braun, *Wayward Technology* (Westport: Greenwood, 1984), 1-38.

20   Kaczynski portrays technology as a kind of addiction: "Never forget that the human race with technology is just like an alcoholic with a barrel of wine." (203)

21   Sometimes the two chief evils are combined in the figure of "industrial-technological society" (77, 114). On occasion Kaczynski points to "science and technology" as his targets (87) and cautions that "science marches on blindly" (92). At times the indictment extends to "civilized societies" as a whole (58). In many other instances his critique is even more abstract, holding

a vague notion of "the system" responsible for the dire state of the world; indeed mantra-like invocations of this undefined term recur throughout the Manifesto (references to "the system" at 119, 129, 139, 162, 163, 164, 175, among others).

22 See also 157: "Assuming that industrial society survives, it is likely that technology will eventually acquire something approaching complete control over human behavior."

23 This is the basic import of Freud's *Civilization and its Discontents*, which many latter-day primitivists oddly invoke as part of their anti-civilization stance. Kaczynski does not engage the question of which sorts of regulation are necessary to social life and which merely reinforce unjust power relations; he does not entertain the possibility of an important distinction between legitimate sublimation and "surplus repression." See Herbert Marcuse, *Eros and Civilization: A Philosophical Inquiry into Freud* (Boston: Beacon, 1955).

24 At one point Kaczynski does appear to recognize the underlying principle of social life: "Since the beginning of civilization, organized societies have had to put pressures on human beings for the sake of the functioning of the social organism." (143) But he seems to resent this fundamental fact about human existence and wish that it might miraculously be suspended. Sociality figures not as a positive good but as a burden, a hindrance to individual liberty. The Manifesto implicitly denies the possibility that "organized society" might be a condition of freedom, and the autonomous regulation of impulses one of the bases of collective self-control and self-management, an expression of social freedom rather than a frustration of it.

25 Kaczynski does not reflect on the strange contradiction involved in this juxtaposition of role models; the success of the frontiersmen he admires came at the price of the annihilation of the indigenous

inhabitants, themselves shining examples, in his portrait, of the Romanticized image of primitive peoples.

26 See also 197-198 on primitive vs. modern forms of power over nature. For a more complex view of primitive societies compare Paul Radin, *Primitive Man as Philosopher* (New York: Dover, 1927); Dorothy Lee, *Freedom and Culture* (New York: Spectrum, 1959); Stanley Diamond, *In Search of the Primitive* (New Brunswick: Transaction, 1974); Pierre Clastres, *Society Against the State* (New York: Zone, 1987).

27 This element in Kaczynski's argument displays striking parallels with the work of Italian fascist theorist Julius Evola (1898-1974); see among others Evola, *Revolt Against the Modern World* (Rochester: Inner Traditions, 1995); Evola, *Men Among the Ruins* (Rochester: Inner Traditions, 2002); Evola, *Pagan Imperialism* (Gornahoor Press, 2017).

28 See also Note 6 on "excessive sex" and associated "perversions." Kaczynski appears to consider "transsexuality" a problem as well (45). For a critique of this approach to "natural human impulses" as a template for social norms see Roger Lancaster, *The Trouble with Nature* (Berkeley: University of California Press, 2003).

29 See also Note 13 for brief criticism of free-market conservatives.

30 The Manifesto uses the term "wild nature" in multiple contexts; see e.g. 5, 177, 183, 214, Note 22, etc. There is a certain ambivalence to the Manifesto's treatment of science, and it is difficult not to read a trace of autobiographical bitterness into some of its remarks on this score. Consider the following plaintive passage in light of Kaczynski's own childhood as a mathematical prodigy sent off to Harvard on scholarship at the age of sixteen: "For example, the system needs scientists, mathematicians and engineers. It can't function without them. So heavy pressure is put on children to

excel in these fields. It isn't natural for an adolescent human being to spend the bulk of his time sitting at a desk absorbed in study. A normal adolescent wants to spend his time in active contact with the real world. […] Among the American Indians, for example, boys were trained in active outdoor pursuits—just the sort of things that boys like. But in our society children are pushed into studying technical subjects, which most do grudgingly." (115)

31 Georges Sorel, *Reflections on Violence* (New York: Collier, 1950). For background see Irving Louis Horowitz, *Radicalism and the Revolt Against Reason: The Social Theories of Georges Sorel* (London: Routledge, 1961), and Zeev Sternhell, *Neither Right nor Left: Fascist Ideology in France* (Princeton: Princeton University Press, 1996).

32 Walter Benjamin, *Selected Writings* volume I (Cambridge: Harvard University Press, 1996), 236-53; see also Michael Löwy, "Walter Benjamin's Critique of Technology" in Löwy, *On Changing the World: Essays in Political Philosophy from Karl Marx to Walter Benjamin* (London: Humanities Press, 1993).

33 For historical overviews see the chapter on "Terrorism and Propaganda by the Deed" in James Joll, *The Anarchists* (New York: Grosset and Dunlap, 1964), and the collection edited by Philippe Kellermann, *Die Propaganda der Tat: Standpunkte und Debatten (1877-1929)* (Münster: Unrast, 2016). There is also a venerable lineage of anarchist pacifism.

34 Letter to *New York Times* postmarked June 21, 1993; letter to *New York Times* April 20, 1995; quoted in Graysmith, *Unabomber*, 259 and 296. Scott Corey situates the Manifesto within the tradition of "revolutionary anarchism" while noting its anarcho-individualist orientation in contrast to social anarchist tendencies; cf. Corey, "On the Unabomber," 157 and 169-71.

35 For comparison to Kaczynski's fragmentary appropriation of

anarchist themes in the service of his longed-for revolution against technology, see the sophisticated discussion of technological knowledge and state hegemony in James Scott, *Seeing Like a State* (New Haven: Yale University Press, 1998), particularly 311-33.

36 Examples include Bob Black, *Anarchy After Leftism* (Columbia: C.A.L. Press, 1997), and the periodical *Anarchy: A Journal of Desire Armed*. Black contends that the Unabomber represents "the best and the predominant thinking in contemporary North American anarchism" (quoted in John Zerzan, *Running on Emptiness: The Pathology of Civilization*, Los Angeles: Feral House, 2002, 153). For a contrary view see Wayne Price, "Is the Unabomber an Anarchist?" *Love and Rage* September 1995.

37 See the exchange on "Post-Left Anarchy" in *Anarchy: A Journal of Desire Armed* no. 57, Spring/Summer 2004, 50-70. An extended critique of "post-left" anarchism from a left anarchist perspective can be found in Peter Staudenmaier, "Anarchists in Wonderland: The Topsy-Turvy World of Post-Left Anarchy" (Institute for Anarchist Studies, 2003). Kaczynski, *Technological Slavery*, 356 fully endorses the 'beyond left and right' stance.

38 Cf. "Two, Three, Many Unabombers" *Anarchy* no. 46, Fall/Winter 1998; "He Means It. Do You?" *Anarchy* no. 44, Fall/Winter 1997. An important exception in this regard is David Watson, a.k.a. George Bradford, the leading theorist at the anarchist journal *The Fifth Estate*, which since the 1970s has developed a complex variation on anarchist critiques of technology. For an example of Watson's early work see George Bradford, "Technology: A System of Domination" *Fifth Estate* Winter 1984. The journal was an important early forum for anarcho-primitivist author John Zerzan and may have helped shape Kaczynski's thinking as well. After the

Manifesto appeared, Watson wrote a lengthy critique of its core ideas: "The Unabomber and the Future of Industrial Society" in David Watson, *Against the Megamachine* (New York: Autonomedia, 1997), 252-68. Neither disavowing nor revising his own contributions, Watson denied that the *Fifth Estate* had a discernible influence on Kaczynski's theories, asserting that "neither the Unabomber's language nor his strategy resembled the FE's work" (258). For context see Steve Millett, "Technology is capital: *Fifth Estate*'s critique of the megamachine" in Jonathan Purkis, ed., *Changing Anarchism: Anarchist Theory and Practice in a Global Age* (Manchester: Manchester University Press, 2004), 73-98.

39 Though primitivist anarchists and "post-left" anarchists overlap, they are distinct currents; see e.g. Jason McQuinn, "Why I am not a Primitivist" *Anarchy* no. 51, Spring/Summer 2001. Alongside and against the anti-left and primitivist strands of contemporary North American anarchism, there is a longstanding tradition of ecological thinking within the historical anarchist movement running from figures like Kropotkin and Reclus to Bookchin. For the German context see Ulrich Linse, *Ökopax und Anarchie: Eine Geschichte der ökologischen Bewegungen in Deutschland* (Munich: Deutscher Taschenbuch Verlag, 1986).

40 The following journals, now largely defunct, offer representative viewpoints: *Green Anarchy* (Eugene, Oregon), which described itself as "an anti-civilization journal of theory and action"; *Green Anarchist* (London, England); *Live Wild Or Die; The Final Days; Species Traitor; Feral: A Journal Towards Wildness*. Aspects of the anarcho-primitivist perspective were also developed in *Earth First!* and *The Fifth Estate* as well as *Anarchy: A Journal of Desire Armed*. Zerzan's books include *Elements of Refusal* (Seattle: Left Bank, 1988), *Future Primitive* (New York: Autonomedia, 1994), and *The*

Stand Against Civilization (Port Townsend: Feral House, 2015), as well as the anthologies *Questioning Technology* (Philadelphia: New Society, 1991) and *Against Civilization* (Eugene: Uncivilized, 1999). Zerzan's statements of the primitivist position include "Why Primitivism?" *Anarchy* no. 56, Fall/Winter 2003, and "Twilight of the Machines" *Anarchy* no. 54, Winter 2002. For social anarchist critiques of anarcho-primitivism see Brian Sheppard, *Anarchism vs. Primitivism* (Tucson: See Sharp, 2003); Charles Thorpe and Ian Welsh, "Beyond primitivism: Towards a twenty-first century anarchist theory and praxis for science and technology" *Anarchist Studies* vol. 16 no. 1 (2008), 48-75.

41 See e.g. Zerzan's 1995 essay "Whose Unabomber?" reprinted in *Running on Emptiness*, 151-55. In the same book Zerzan provides a detailed account of his relationship to Kaczynski (187-93), noting his "heavy emotional identification" with the imprisoned bomber (189). Zerzan dedicated the second edition of his book *Elements of Refusal* (Columbia: C.A.L. Press, 1999) to Kaczynski.

42 Cf. Zerzan's early essays "Industrialism and Domestication" and "The Refusal of Technology" in *Elements of Refusal*, as well as Wolfi Landstreicher, "How then Do We Go Wild?" *Anarchy* no. 52, Fall/Winter 2001. The Unabomber Manifesto gestures toward a critique of domestication in paragraphs 174-175.

43 See Zerzan, "It's All Coming Down!" *Green Anarchy* no. 8, Spring 2002. p. 3. A thoughtful and historically informed examination of the development of Zerzan's ideas is available in the dissertation by Spencer Sunshine, "Post-1960 U.S. Anarchism and Social Theory" (CUNY Graduate Center 2013), 61-70. Sunshine points out that in addition to various forms of Marxism, "one of the main influences on Zerzan was the interwar German right." (69)

44 April 20, 1995 letter to the *Times* quoted in Graysmith,

Unabomber, 296. Kaczynski was apparently an avid reader of the anarchist and radical environmentalist press, and some of these periodicals may have influenced his choice of targets; see e.g. Graysmith, *Unabomber*, 280 and 426, and Foster, *Author Unknown*, 136. On Kaczynski's relationship with radical environmentalist activism see Bron Taylor, "Religion, Violence and Radical Environmentalism: From Earth First! to the Unabomber to the Earth Liberation Movement" *Terrorism and Political Violence* vol. 10 no. 4 (1998), 1-42.

45 Kaczynski attempted to correspond with parts of the anarcho-primitivist milieu even before the Manifesto was published; cf. Chase, *Harvard and the Unabomber*, 77. He continued this correspondence during his imprisonment; see e.g. Kaczynski's letter to the editors, *Live Wild or Die* no. 7, Spring 1998, and the substantial interview "Ted Speaks" in *Green Anarchist* no. 57, Autumn 1999. After a falling out with Zerzan, Kaczynski came to reject the primitivist paradigm; see his expansive critique of anarcho-primitivism in Kaczynski, *Technological Slavery*, 128-89.

46 Ted Kaczynski, untitled 1971 typescript, p. 1; a photographic reproduction of the twenty-three page document appears in Graysmith, *Unabomber*, 488-510. In it Kaczynski warns against "genetic engineering" (8-10) and concludes with a call for "stopping federal aid to scientific research." (23)

47 *Green Anarchy* no. 7, Fall/Winter 2001, 5.

48 Ted Kaczynski, "Hit Where It Hurts" *Green Anarchy* no. 8, Spring 2002. Kaczynski's piece was the lead article in this issue of the premier primitivist journal, beginning on the top of p. 1 and continuing on pp. 18-19. The editorial collective noted their partial disagreement with the article (particularly "Ted's hostility towards feminism") in an addendum on p. 19. Four years

later Kaczynski criticized *Green Anarchy* in a lengthy interview with *Anarchy: A Journal of Desire Armed*; see "Ted Kaczynski Interview" *Anarchy* no. 61, Spring 2006, 37-43.

49 Kaczynski, "Hit Where It Hurts," 1.

50 Kaczynski, "Hit Where It Hurts," 18.

51 The Unabomber Manifesto similarly emphasizes the dangers of "genetic engineering" and "the immense power of biotechnology" in paragraph 124; this appears to be a consistent theme throughout Kaczynski's various writings. For a contrasting range of radical critiques of biotechnology see Brian Tokar, ed., *Redesigning Life? The Worldwide Challenge to Genetic Engineering* (London: Zed, 2001).

52 Kaczynski, "Hit Where It Hurts," 19.

53 Tim Luke reads the Manifesto as congruent with Mumford's work (Luke, "Re-Reading the Unabomber Manifesto," 87), while Scott Corey emphasizes Kaczynski's debt to Ellul (Corey, "On the Unabomber," 159). Both authors are treated at length in Langdon Winner's superb intellectual history *Autonomous Technology: Technics-out-of-Control as a Theme in Political Thought* (Cambridge: MIT Press, 1977). Mumford and Ellul are also discussed extensively in Nicols Fox's celebration of neo-Luddite attitudes, *Against the Machine* (Washington: Island Press, 2002). Kaczynski's brother David reports that Ellul's book *The Technological Society* was Ted's "bible" (Graysmith, *Unabomber*, 394). In 1985 Ted wrote to David: "You'll recall how pleased I was when I encountered Jacques Ellul's book, *The Technological Society*, because his thinking ran so close to my own." (Quoted in Foster, *Author Unknown*, 139) Kaczynski cited the book in his untitled 1971 essay, p. 10; cf. Graysmith, *Unabomber*, 497.

54 Lewis Mumford, *Technics and Civilization* (New York: Harcourt,

1934).

55 Lewis Mumford, *The Myth of the Machine* (New York: Harcourt, 1967). Here Mumford wrote, in direct contradiction to the Manifesto's fundamental themes, "I submit that at every stage man's inventions and transformations were less for the purpose of increasing the food supply or controlling nature than for utilizing his own immense organic resources and expressing his latent potentialities." (8) "At its point of origin, technics was related to the whole nature of man, and that nature played a part in every aspect of industry: thus technics, at the beginning, was broadly life-centered, not work-centered or power-centered. As in any other ecological complex, varied human interests and purposes, different organic needs, restrained the overgrowth of any single component." (9)

56 Mumford, *The Myth of the Machine*, 10.

57 Mumford attributed major technological shifts to "social organization," not to "mechanical inventions," and had a dialectical conception of the intertwining of "positive" and "negative" aspects of the rise of large-scale technology (*The Myth of the Machine*, 11, 259), while flatly rejecting the notion that "civilization inexorably develops in this fashion" (Mumford, *Art and Technics*, New York: Columbia University Press, 1952, 156).

58 Jacques Ellul, *The Technological Society* (New York: Vintage, 1964), 87.

59 Ellul, *The Technological Society*, 29, 42.

60 Ellul, *The Technological Society*, 128, 126, 93.

61 Ellul, *The Technological Society*, 141.

62 Ellul, *Autopsy of Revolution* (New York: Knopf, 1971), 275. For further discussion of Ellul's views on technology see Detlev Langenegger, *Gesamtdeutungen moderner Technik* (Würzburg: Königshausen & Neumann, 1990), 105-84.

63 Ellul, *Anarchy and Christianity* (Grand Rapids: Eerdmans, 1991), 11.

See also Ellul, *Violence: Reflections from a Christian Perspective* (New York: Seabury, 1969). The Unabomber Manifesto acknowledges that some other anarchists would reject Kaczynski's violent tactics; see Note 34.

64 Luke, "Re-Reading the Unabomber Manifesto," 83; three paragraphs later he reiterates that Kaczynski's argument "parallels Marcuse's account of technology" (84).

65 See e.g. "Nature and Revolution" in Herbert Marcuse, *Counterrevolution and Revolt*; "The Problem of Violence and the Radical Opposition" and "Freedom and Freud's Theory of Instincts" in Marcuse, *Five Lectures*; "On Hedonism" in Marcuse, *Negations*; "Some Social Implications of Modern Technology" in Marcuse, *Technology, War and Fascism*; as well as Marcuse, *An Essay on Liberation* and Marcuse, *Eros and Civilization*. For further discussion compare C. Fred Alford, *Science and the Revenge of Nature: Marcuse and Habermas* (Gainesville: University Press of Florida, 1985); Andrew Feenberg, "Marcuse and the Critique of Technology: From Dystopia to Interaction" in Feenberg, *Alternative Modernity: The Technical Turn in Philosophy and Social Science* (Berkeley: University of California Press, 1995); and Samir Gandesha, "Marcuse, Habermas, and the Critique of Technology" in John Abromeit, ed., *Herbert Marcuse: A Critical Reader* (New York: Routledge, 2004).

66 Herbert Marcuse, *One-Dimensional Man* (Boston: Beacon, 1964), 18.

67 Marcuse, *One-Dimensional Man*, 18, 227. In a complete reversal of Kaczynski's stance, Marcuse pointed to automation as a route toward freedom and away from technological subjugation (37), and speculated that "mechanization and standardization may one day help to shift the center of gravity from the necessities of material production to the arena of free human realization." (160)

68 Marcuse, *One-Dimensional Man*, 233, 235.

69 Kaczynski seems to have had no affiliations whatsoever to the New Left. He spent the 1960s at Harvard, the University of Michigan, and Berkeley, yet was apparently never involved in any of the radical movements of the era. For his retrospective account of his political views at the time see Kaczynski, *Technological Slavery*, 388: "I've never had anything but contempt for the so-called '60s kids,' the radicals of the Vietnam-War era. [...] I was a supporter of the Vietnam War." Kaczynski's sometime associate Zerzan, a former leftist, now identifies himself straightforwardly as an anti-leftist; see John Zerzan, "Post-Leftists! One more Effort if you would be Anti-Leftist!" *Anarchy* no. 58, Fall 2004, 64.

70 Neither Luke nor Corey in their *Telos* articles discusses the tradition of German right-wing critiques of technology, and neither mentions Klages, Spengler, or Jünger. Kaczynski's fellow anti-civilization enthusiasts are not so circumspect. Zerzan invokes both Spengler and Jünger in support of his own arguments; see Zerzan, "Twilight of the Machines," 38-39; Zerzan, *Running on Emptiness*, 153; Zerzan, *Questioning Technology*, 217; Zerzan, *Future Primitive Revisited* (Port Townsend: Feral House, 2012), 143 and 160-61. The opening editorial in *Green Anarchy* no. 11, Winter 2003, 2, begins with a quote from Spengler, and Spengler is positively invoked in issue no. 17, Summer 2004, as well.

71 Though the possibility is not far-fetched; Kaczynski knows German and seems to have read widely in the critical literature on technology. References to Klages, Spengler, or Jünger do not appear in his published works.

72 For useful introductions to this intellectual context see Kurt Sontheimer's classic study *Antidemokratisches Denken in*

der Weimarer Republik (Munich: Nymphenburger, 1962), in particular 48-58, 65-72, 322-26, and Stefan Breuer, *Ordnungen der Ungleichheit: Die deutsche Rechte im Widerstreit ihrer Ideen 1871-1945* (Darmstadt: Wissenschaftliche Buchgesellschaft, 2001), with references to Klages, Spengler, and F.G. Jünger throughout. Anne Harrington has aptly described *Lebensphilosophie* or 'life philosophy' as "the somewhat inchoate and scattered intellectual movement of the postwar years that aimed collectively to demand that the whole Enlightenment tradition responsible for the Machine in all of its faces now stand up and prove its legitimacy against Life" (Harrington, *Reenchanted Science: Holism in German Culture from Wilhelm II to Hitler*, Princeton University Press 1996, 32).

73 On the intense debates surrounding these topics at the time see Friedrich Dessauer, *Streit um die Technik* (Bonn: Cohen, 1928). The fourth edition (Frankfurt 1956) includes an extensive bibliography of German-language literature on technology from 1807 until 1956. Proponents of far right ecology in twenty-first century Germany point to Klages and F.G. Jünger as their forebears; see e.g. Norbert Borrmann, "Ökologie ist rechts" *Sezession* October 2013, 4-7. On the Italian right, Julius Evola displayed a particular interest in both Spengler and Klages, and translated Spengler's *Decline of the West* into Italian.

74 Ludwig Klages, *Mensch und Erde* (Jena: Diederichs, 1929); see repeated references to "Wissenschaft" and "Technik," 1-2 and 12. The essay is available in English translation from the far right publisher Arktos: Ludwig Klages, "Man and Earth" in Klages, *The Biocentric Worldview* (London: Arktos, 2013), 26-44. For background see Martin Kagel, "Widersacher des Fortschritts: Zu Ludwig Klages' ökologischem Manifest 'Mensch und Erde'" in Jost Hermand, ed., *Mit den Bäumen sterben die Menschen: Zur*

Kulturgeschichte der Ökologie (Cologne: Böhlau, 1993), 199-220;
Joachim Radkau, *The Age of Ecology: A Global History* (Cambridge:
Polity, 2014), 28-32.

75 Klages, *Mensch und Erde*, 3-7, 10, 16.

76 Klages, *Mensch und Erde*, 4, 20. For further discussion of Klages'
views on technology see Gerd-Klaus Kaltenbrunner, "Vom
Weltschmerz des technischen Zeitalters: Ludwig Klages" in Karl
Schwedhelm, ed, *Propheten des Nationalismus* (Munich: List, 1969),
and Nitzan Lebovic, *The Philosophy of Life and Death: Ludwig Klages
and the Rise of a Nazi Biopolitics* (New York: Palgrave, 2013). His
ecological outlook continues to find admirers on the far right; as an
example see Reinhard Falter, *Ludwig Klages: Lebensphilosophie als
Zivilisationskritik* (Neustadt: Arnshaugk, 2015).

77 Oswald Spengler, *Der Mensch und die Technik: Beitrag zu einer
Philosophie des Lebens* (Munich: Beck, 1931); English translation
Man and Technics: A Contribution to a Philosophy of Life (London:
Allen & Unwin, 1932). Rolf Peter Sieferle notes that part of the
book's argument proceeds "in the footsteps of Ludwig Klages"
(Sieferle, *Die Konservative Revolution*, Frankfurt: Fischer 1995,
119), while Gilbert Merlio observes that "some passages in *Man and
Technics* seem to be directly copied from Klages" (Merlio, "Kultur-
und Technikkritik vor und nach dem ersten Weltkrieg" in Friedrich
Strack, ed., *Titan Technik: Ernst und Friedrich Georg Jünger über das
technische Zeitalter*, Würzburg: Königshausen & Neumann 2000,
37). For further background see Detlef Felken, *Oswald Spengler:
Konservativer Denker zwischen Kaiserreich und Diktatur* (Munich:
Beck, 1988), especially 177-83 on *Der Mensch und die Technik*.
Felken locates this work in the tradition of "Lebensphilosophie
naturalism" (178) and notes its "biologistic implications" (179).

78 Jeffrey Herf's reading of *Man and Technics*, for example, is

diametrically opposed to the reading I will present here. Herf asserts that Spengler "wrote *Man and Technics* to establish his protechnological credentials." (Herf, *Reactionary Modernism: Technology, Culture, and Politics in Weimar and the Third Reich*, Cambridge University Press 1984, 38) Herf further argues that in Spengler's view technological advances "expand human freedom." (ibid. 65) Dina Gusejnova similarly sees an "endorsement of technological progress" in *Man and Technics*: Gusejnova, "Concepts of culture and technology in Germany, 1916-1933: Ernst Cassirer and Oswald Spengler" *Journal of European Studies* vol. 36 no. 1 (2006), 5-30, quote at 12. There are undoubtedly ambivalent elements in Spengler's book, but in my view such claims are incompatible with the text itself. For interpretations of *Man and Technics* that are contrary to Herf's and Gusejnova's see Ernst Bloch, *Heritage of Our Times* (Berkeley: University of California Press, 1991), 291-92; Winner, *Autonomous Technology*, 145-46; Pierre Bourdieu, *The Political Ontology of Martin Heidegger* (Stanford University Press, 1991), 16-17; cf. also Theodor Adorno's brief critical review of Spengler's book from 1932: "Oswald Spengler, Der Mensch und die Technik" in Adorno, *Vermischte Schriften* I (Frankfurt: Suhrkamp, 1986), 197-99.

79 Spengler, *Man and Technics*, 43; I have retained the characteristic typography of the original English translation (for example, "Nature" is capitalized throughout) while occasionally modifying the wording; cf. Spengler, *Der Mensch und die Technik*, 34. More concretely, Spengler warns against deforestation, climate change, and the extinction of animal species in terms similar to Klages (*Man and Technics*, 94; *Der Mensch und die Technik*, 78). On Spengler's early concerns about deforestation see Oswald Spengler, *Spengler Letters* (London: Allen and Unwin, 1966), 129-30.

80 Spengler, *Man and Technics*, 44; *Der Mensch und die Technik*, 35. He goes on to describe machines as "weapons against Nature" (*Man and Technics*, 88; *Der Mensch und die Technik*, 73). For a salutary contrast to Spengler's narrative of the "revenge of Nature" (*Man and Technics*, 69) see Max Horkheimer, "The Revolt of Nature" in Horkheimer, *Eclipse of Reason* (New York: Oxford University Press, 1947).

81 Spengler, *Man and Technics*, 50; *Der Mensch und die Technik*, 38. John Zerzan proposes a similar theory of agriculture as the original misstep; see "Agriculture" in Zerzan, *Elements of Refusal*. See also Spengler's critique of "domestication" (*Man and Technics*, 61; *Der Mensch und die Technik*, 48). For Spengler's warnings against increasing population see *Man and Technics*, 69-70; *Der Mensch und die Technik*, 56.

82 Spengler, *Man and Technics*, 76; *Der Mensch und die Technik*, 61; emphasis (as always) in original.

83 Spengler, *Man and Technics*, 66, 69; *Der Mensch und die Technik*, 52-53, 55-56. In a further parallel to the Manifesto, Spengler argues that there are two kinds of people, "men whose nature is to command and men whose nature is to obey" (*Man and Technics*, 63; *Der Mensch und die Technik*, 50), emphasizing that the few leaders and many followers are born to their station (*Man and Technics*, 92; *Der Mensch und die Technik*, 77). In Kaczynski's words, "The majority of people are natural followers, not leaders" (Note 5); see also his distinction between "intelligent" people (187) and "the unthinking majority" (188).

84 Spengler, *Man and Technics*, 93-94; *Der Mensch und die Technik*, 78-79.

85 Spengler, *Man and Technics*, 97, 102; *Der Mensch und die Technik*, 82, 87. Adorno's early review of the book offers a condensed and incisive critique of this fatalism, noting that in Spengler's narrative, technology has been "rendered absolute," "without even raising the question of whether technology's autonomy from its social use

could be corrected by changing the social structure." Adorno, *Vermischte Schriften*, 198. Racial themes play a conspicuous if subordinate role in Spengler's book; see e.g. *Der Mensch und die Technik*, 54, 65, 70, 86. The passages are somewhat muted in the English edition, where the term "Rasse" becomes "breed"; cf. *Man and Technics*, 67, 80, 85, 101.

86 Friedrich Georg Jünger, *Die Perfektion der Technik* (Frankfurt: Klostermann, 1946). The original 1939 manuscript bore the title *Die Illusionen der Technik*. The English translation is titled *The Failure of Technology: Perfection Without Purpose* (Chicago: Regnery, 1949). Jünger wrote two further books on the theme: *Maschine und Eigentum* (Frankfurt 1949) and *Die vollkommene Schöpfung: Natur oder Naturwissenschaft?* (Frankfurt 1969). Written mainly in 1939, with an epilogue added in 1946, *Die Perfektion der Technik* was a reversal from Jünger's 1926 manifesto *Der Aufmarsch des Nationalismus*, which had been basically pro-technological in the same vein as his brother's work of the period. For his perspective in the Nazi era see Friedrich Georg Jünger, "Über die technische Perfektion" *Deutsches Volkstum: Monatsschrift für das deutsche Geistesleben* January 1941, 9-13.

87 There is an extensive literature on both brothers; on the question of technology see the collection edited by Strack, *Titan Technik*, which offers a variety of viewpoints sympathetic toward the Jüngers, as well as Daniel Morat, *Von der Tat zur Gelassenheit: Konservatives Denken bei Martin Heidegger, Ernst Jünger und Friedrich Georg Jünger 1920-1960* (Göttingen: Wallstein, 2007). For an early overview of Ernst Jünger's approach to technology, framed within a broader perspective on Jünger as a "conservative anarchist," see Hans-Peter Schwarz, *Der konservative Anarchist: Politik und Zeitkritik Ernst Jüngers* (Freiburg: Rombach, 1962),

chapter 7, "Über die Technik," 189-205.

88 Even Ernst Jünger's views were not as consistently pro-technological as they are sometimes depicted. See, for example, his 1933 essay "Die Technik und ihre Zuordnung" (published less than a year after *Der Arbeiter*), reprinted in Strack, *Titan Technik*, 291-95. The essay adopts a notably ambivalent attitude toward "die Technik" and its impact on the individual, as well as toward the future of technological society. Ernst Jünger's later work took a decidedly pessimistic turn on the question of technology; in *Aladins Problem* (Stuttgart: Klett-Cotta, 1983), 64 he wrote: "I have been convinced for years that we live in a desert, and that technology increasingly contributes to the monotony and extent of this desert." His change of heart can be traced in part to his exchanges with his brother and with their mutual friend Martin Heidegger. For a recent re-appraisal see Oliver Jahraus, "Der verkannte Vordenker: Ernst Jünger und die Grünen" *Kursbuch* March 2019, 64-78.

89 Jünger, *The Failure of Technology*, 8; *Die Perfektion der Technik*, 7. Later in the book, Jünger distances his own analysis from "the romantic rejection of technology" (*Failure of Technology*, 141; *Perfektion der Technik*, 161).

90 Jünger, *The Failure of Technology*, 9, 17; *Die Perfektion der Technik*, 9, 17. He also notes that "technical progress has enriched a small and not always pleasant group of industrialists, entrepreneurs, and inventors" (12).

91 Jünger, *The Failure of Technology*, 20; *Die Perfektion der Technik*, 19. He also states categorically that "technology" is "filled with destructive forces." (*Failure of Technology*, 118; *Perfektion der Technik*, 142)

92 Jünger, *The Failure of Technology*, 21, 164; *Die Perfektion der Technik*, 21, 182.

93   Jünger, *The Failure of Technology*, 126; *Die Perfektion der Technik*, 148. Jünger distinguishes between "people" and "the masses" (*Volk* and *Masse*), the former a positive category, the latter a negative one (*Failure of Technology*, 132; *Perfektion der Technik*, 154). The corresponding distinction in Spengler is between "personality" and "mass" (*Persönlichkeit* and *Masse*): Spengler, *Man and Technics*, 71; *Der Mensch und die Technik*, 58.

94   Jünger, *The Failure of Technology*, 164; *Die Perfektion der Technik*, 181.

95   Jünger, *Die Perfektion der Technik*, 32; cf. *The Failure of Technology*, 31. Jünger shared several of Kaczynski's other preoccupations, bemoaning "the emancipation of women" (*Failure of Technology*, 180; *Perfektion der Technik*, 203) and warning against "technical organization" that is "subsidized by the state" (Jünger, *Die vollkommene Schöpfung*, 10).

96   Houston Stewart Chamberlain, *The Foundations of the Nineteenth Century* (London: Lane, 1912), 363-64; see also Chamberlain, *Natur und Leben* (Munich: Bruckmann, 1928). Further examples of the genre include Alfred Böttcher, *Das Scheinglück der Technik* (Weimar 1932); Paul Krannhals, *Das organische Weltbild* (Munich 1928); and the works of Raoul Francé, such as *Aphorismen zu einer Natur- und Lebensphilosophie* (Zurich 1908); *Die Harmonie in der Natur* (Stuttgart 1926); *Welt, Erde und Menschheit* (Berlin 1928). For post-war continuations of this tradition see Werner Haverbeck, *Das Ziel der Technik* (Olten 1965), and Haverbeck, *Die andere Schöpfung* (Stuttgart 1978).

97   Martin Heidegger, "The Question Concerning Technology" in Heidegger, *Basic Writings* (New York: Harper, 1977), 311. On the relation between Heidegger's and Friedrich Georg Jünger's approaches to technology see Langenegger, *Gesamtdeutungen moderner Technik*, 197-98 and 213-15. Comparable ideas are

evident in Ernst Niekisch's 1931 essay "Menschenfresser Technik" ("the cannibalism of technology") and his later article "Technik und Natur."

98 A further factor that complicates any easy categorization of such perspectives into left and right variants is the persistence of personal and intellectual continuities between the two camps, a dynamic that is perhaps most notable in the case of Heidegger's erstwhile student Marcuse.

99 See Foster, *Author Unknown*, 138 on the parallels to contemporary American conservative pundits in Kaczynski's style and vocabulary.

100 Mark Neocleous, *Fascism* (Minneapolis: University of Minnesota Press, 1997), 87.

101 Marco Armiero and Wilko Graf von Hardenberg, "Green Rhetoric in Blackshirts: Italian Fascism and the Environment" *Environment and History* vol. 19 no 3 (2013) summarize the situation in Fascist Italy as follows: "Nature conservation showed itself in a plurality of forms, seldom respectful of ecological relationships within the natural world, but always structured as an attempt to bring a 'civilised' nature nearer to the people." (311) There were of course exceptions; a Fascist attack on "the myth of the machine" in an explicitly racist context can be found in Massimo Scaligero, *La Razza di Roma* (Rome: Mantero, 1939), 170-73. For surveys of this contentious theme see Eric Brose, "Generic Fascism Revisited: Attitudes toward Technology in Germany and Italy, 1919-1945" *German Studies Review* vol. 10 no. 2 (1987), 273-97; Peter Staudenmaier, "Fascism" in Shepard Krech III and Carolyn Merchant, editors, *Encyclopedia of World Environmental History* vol. 2 (New York: Routledge, 2004), 517-21; John Guse, "Nazi technical thought revisited" *History and Technology* vol. 26 no. 1 (2010), 3-33.

102 On "neither Right nor Left" as a classic fascist slogan see Robert

Paxton, *The Anatomy of Fascism* (New York: Knopf, 2004), 11-12, as well as the provocative exploration of this background in Sternhell, *Neither Right nor Left*, and Steve Bastow and James Martin, *Third Way Discourse: European Ideologies in the Twentieth Century* (Edinburgh University Press 2003), 93-116. Herbert Gruhl, one of the conservative founders of the German Greens, introduced this phrase into green politics at the beginning of the 1980s before leaving the Greens to found a series of far-right ecological parties.

103 For an illuminating contrast to Kaczynski see Cornelius Castoriadis' profound meditation on *techne* and its historical transformations in Castoriadis, *Crossroads in the Labyrinth* (Cambridge: MIT Press, 1984), 229-59, as well as Castoriadis, "Dead End?" in Castoriadis, *Philosophy, Politics, Autonomy* (Oxford University Press 1991).

104 "The Luddites," writes David Noble, "were not against technology per se. They were contending with the social relations of industrial capitalism" (Noble, *Progress Without People: In Defense of Luddism*, Chicago: Kerr 1993, 35). Tellingly, there is no critique of capitalism anywhere in the Unabomber Manifesto.

105 In the words of Arnold Pacey, "technology is partly an expression of the values and aspirations of the people who create and use it." Pacey, *The Maze of Ingenuity: Ideas and Idealism in the Development of Technology* (New York: Holmes & Meier, 1975), 14.

106 Winner, *Autonomous Technology*, 325. This social specificity is lost on Kaczynski: "To relieve the pressure on nature it is not necessary to create a special kind of social system, it is only necessary to get rid of industrial society." (184)

107 There is one brief moment in the Manifesto that acknowledges a possible differentiation. At paragraph 208 in a 232 paragraph essay, Kaczynski writes: "We distinguish between two kinds

of technology, which we will call small-scale technology and
organization-dependent technology." While this concession is
an improvement on the document's otherwise across the board
dismissal of technology as such, the distinction Kaczynski
draws here depends on precarious assumptions about social
organization and scale, and in any case plays no appreciable role
in the rest of his analysis.

108 For an ecological-anarchist exploration of these possibilities
see Murray Bookchin, "The Social Matrix of Technology" in
Bookchin, *The Ecology of Freedom: The Emergence and Dissolution
of Hierarchy* (Palo Alto: Cheshire, 1982), as well as Bookchin,
"The Concept of Ecotechnologies and Ecocommunities" and
"Self-Management and the New Technology" in Bookchin,
Toward an Ecological Society (Montreal: Black Rose, 1980).
Bookchin was an early critic of Ellul's *Technological Society*
and Jünger's *Failure of Technology*, noting that "Both Juenger
and Elul believe that the debasement of man by the machine is
intrinsic to the development of technology": Murray Bookchin,
"Towards a Liberatory Technology" in Bookchin, *Post-Scarcity
Anarchism* (Berkeley: Ramparts, 1971), 86. Innovative readings
of the debate between social ecologists and deep ecologists can
be found in Mark Stoll, "Green versus Green: Religions, Ethics,
and the Bookchin-Foreman Dispute" *Environmental History*
vol. 6 no. 3 (2001), 412-27; Stephen Millett, "Divergence and
Disagreement in Contemporary Anarchist Communism: Social
Ecology and Anarchist Primitivism" (dissertation, University
of Central Lancashire, 2002); Keith Makoto Woodhouse, *The
Ecocentrists: A History of Radical Environmentalism* (New York:
Columbia University Press, 2018); Brian Morris, "Anarchism and
Environmental Philosophy" in Nathan Jun, ed., *Brill's Companion*

to Anarchism and Philosophy (Leiden: Brill, 2018), 369-400.

109 The Manifesto thus fails to capture the complexity of critical reactions to the rise of industrial technology. For a historical overview compare Samuel Hays, *The Response to Industrialism 1885-1914* (University of Chicago Press 1957), and Michael Adas, *Machines as the Measure of Men: Science, Technology, and Ideologies of Western Dominance* (Ithaca: Cornell University Press, 1989).

110 For a variety of perspectives that point in this direction see David Dickson, *The Politics of Alternative Technology* (New York: Universe, 1975); Ynestra King, "Toward an Ecological Feminism and a Feminist Ecology" in Joan Rothschild, ed., *Machina Ex Dea: Feminist Perspectives on Technology* (New York: Pergamon, 1983); Andrew Feenberg, *Critical Theory of Technology* (Oxford University Press 1991); Takis Fotopoulos, "Towards a Democratic Conception of Science and Technology" *Democracy and Nature* no. 10, 1998; John McCormick, ed., *Confronting Mass Democracy and Industrial Technology* (Durham: Duke University Press, 2002).

111 Quoted in Chase, *Harvard and the Unabomber*, 59.

112 Chase, *Harvard and the Unabomber*, 360. Tim Luke notes that the Manifesto's "simplistic construction of 'nature'" comes "straight out of deep ecology." (Luke, "Re-Reading the Unabomber Manifesto," 88) The complex history of shifting conceptions of nature in the Western tradition is examined in R.G. Collingwood, *The Idea of Nature* (Oxford University Press 1960); Clarence Glacken, *Traces on the Rhodian Shore: Nature and Culture in Western Thought from Ancient Times to the End of the Eighteenth Century* (Berkeley: University of California Press, 1967); Raymond Williams, *The Country and the City* (London: Chatto and Windus, 1973); Keith Thomas, *Man and the Natural World: A History of the Modern Sensibility* (New York: Pantheon, 1983); Kate Soper, *What is*

Nature? Culture, Politics and the Non-Human (Oxford: Blackwell, 1995); Carolyn Merchant, *Reinventing Eden: The Fate of Nature in Western Culture* (New York: Routledge, 2013).

113 For a concise statement of this position see Andrew McLaughlin, "The Heart of Deep Ecology" in George Sessions, ed., *Deep Ecology for the Twenty-First Century* (Boston: Shambhala, 1995). John Zerzan, for his part, sharply repudiates the possibility of a transformed technology participating in an "integration between humanity and nature." (Zerzan in *Green Anarchy* no. 14, Fall 2003, 1)

114 A wealth of historical and philosophical literature interrogates the notion of 'wilderness'; cf. Ramachandra Guha, "Radical American Environmentalism and Wilderness Preservation: A Third World Critique" *Environmental Ethics* vol. 11 no.1 (1989), 71-83; Peter Schmitt, *Back to Nature: The Arcadian Myth in Urban America* (Johns Hopkins University Press 1990); Peter van Wyck, *Primitives in the Wilderness: Deep Ecology and the Missing Human Subject* (State University of New York Press 1997); J. Baird Callicott, "Contemporary Criticisms of the Received Wilderness Idea" in David Cole, ed., *Wilderness Science in a Time of Change* (Fort Collins: Rocky Mountain Research Station, 2000), 24-31. The best condensed critique is by environmental historian William Cronon, "The Trouble with Wilderness, or, Getting back to the Wrong Nature" in Cronon, ed., *Uncommon Ground: Toward Reinventing Nature* (New York: Norton, 1995).

115 While Kaczynski does recognize that "even pre-industrial societies can do significant damage to nature" (184), he never examines the presuppositions of his construction of nature in a historically informed way. Cf. William Thomas, ed., *Man's Role in Changing the Face of the Earth* (University of Chicago Press 1956); Neil Evernden, *The Social Creation of Nature* (Johns

Hopkins University Press 1992); William Denevan, "The Pristine Myth: The Landscape of the Americas in 1492" *Annals of the Association of American Geographers* vol. 82 no. 3 (1992), 369-85; Charles Redman, *Human Impact on Ancient Environments* (University of Arizona Press 1999); Stephen Germic, *American Green: Class, Crisis, and the Deployment of Nature in Central Park, Yosemite, and Yellowstone* (Lexington Books 2001); Karl Jacoby, *Crimes Against Nature* (University of California Press 2001); Noel Castree, *Making Sense of Nature* (Routledge 2014).

116 Theodor Adorno, *Ästhetische Theorie* (Frankfurt: Suhrkamp, 1970), 106; cf. Adorno, *Aesthetic Theory* (Minneapolis: University of Minnesota Press, 1997), 68. Building on his critique of the Unabomber Manifesto's precursors, Adorno's analysis anticipates and negates Kaczynski's: "So long as progress, deformed by utilitarianism, does violence to the surface of the earth, it will be impossible – in spite of all proof to the contrary – completely to counter the perception that what antedates the trend is in its backwardness better and more humane. Rationalization is not yet rational; the universality of mediation has yet to be transformed into living life; and this endows the traces of immediacy, however dubious and antiquated, with an element of corrective justice. The longing that is assuaged and betrayed by them and made pernicious through spurious fulfillment is nevertheless legitimated by the denial of gratification continually imposed by the status quo." Adorno, *Aesthetic Theory*, 64.

117 Adorno, *Aesthetic Theory*, 65-68; I have altered Robert Hullot-Kentor's fine translation by rendering "Technik" as "technology" and have drawn on Herbert Marcuse's partial translation as well (see Marcuse, *Counterrevolution and Revolt*, 66); cf. Adorno, *Ästhetische Theorie*, 103-07. Consider also this passage: "For in

every particular aesthetic experience of nature the social whole is
lodged. Society not only provides the schemata of perception but
peremptorily determines what nature means through contrast and
similarity. Experience of nature is co-constituted by the capacity of
determinate negation. With the expansion of technique and, even
more important, the total expansion of the exchange principle,
natural beauty increasingly fulfills a contrasting function and
is thus integrated into the reified world it opposes." (Adorno,
Aesthetic Theory, 68)

118 Against this tradition stand the closing words of Max Horkheimer's
1944 essay "The Revolt of Nature": "In summary, we are the
heirs, for better or worse, of the Enlightenment and technological
progress. To oppose these by regressing to more primitive stages
does not alleviate the permanent crisis they have brought about.
On the contrary, such expedients lead from historically reasonable
to utterly barbaric forms of social domination. The sole way of
assisting nature is to unshackle its seeming opposite, independent
thought." Horkheimer, *Eclipse of Reason*, 127.

119 It is instructive to re-read the Manifesto's candid statement "The
positive ideal that we propose is nature" in light of Adorno's
penetrating criticism of the deceptive simplicity this move
conceals: "If the whole is the spell, the negative, then the negation
of particularities, whose concept consists in that whole, remains
negative. Its positive moment would only be determinate
negation, critique, not a suddenly transformative result that
holds affirmation happily in its hands." (Theodor Adorno,
Negative Dialektik, Frankfurt: Suhrkamp 1966, 161; cf. Adorno,
Negative Dialectics, New York: Continuum 1973, 158-59) See also
Adorno, *Prisms* (Cambridge: MIT Press, 1981), 164: "The whole,
as a positive entity, cannot be antithetically extracted from an

estranged and splintered reality by means of the will and power of the individual; if it is not to degenerate into deception and ideology, it must assume the form of negation."

120 Anthony Rotundo, *American Manhood: Transformations in Masculinity from the Revolution to the Modern Era* (New York: Basic, 1993), 227-32 and 251-54; for the classic study of these myths see Richard Slotkin, *Regeneration through Violence: The Mythology of the American Frontier, 1600-1860* (Wesleyan University Press 1973).

121 Aage Borchgrevink, *A Norwegian Tragedy: Anders Behring Breivik and the Massacre on Utøya* (Cambridge: Polity, 2013), 20-22; Mattias Gardell, "Crusader Dreams: Oslo 22/7, Islamophobia, and the Quest for a Monocultural Europe" *Terrorism and Political Violence* vol. 26 no. 1 (2014), 129-55.

122 See e.g. Paul Kingsnorth, "Dark Ecology" *Orion Magazine* December 20, 2012, reprinted in his 2017 collection *Confessions of a Recovering Environmentalist.* Jensen's case is more complicated. As with Zerzan, Kaczynski's relations with Jensen and his circle have evidently become strained, though ideological commonalities are not difficult to discern. There are also noteworthy differences; for a "Deep Green Resistance" perspective on the history of right-wing ecological politics see *Deep Green Resistance: Strategy to Save the Planet* (New York: Seven Stories, 2011), 115-26.

123 John Richardson, "Children of Ted: The Unlikely New Generation of Unabomber Acolytes" *New York Magazine* December 2018; Jake Hanrahan, "Inside the Unabomber's odd and furious online revival" *Wired* August 1, 2018. Perhaps the clearest successor to Kaczynski is the semi-clandestine (and possibly apocryphal) group calling itself "Individuals Tending Toward the Wild," sometimes rendered "Individualists Tending Toward Savagery"

or ITS, whose early communiqués cited the Manifesto before disavowing Kaczynski. Like many of his comments on kindred contemporaries, Kaczynski's remarks about ITS have been dismissive. See the discussion of ITS in Michael Loadenthal, *The Politics of Attack: Communiqués and Insurrectionary Violence* (Manchester: Manchester University Press, 2017), 84-90.

124 Chaia Heller, *Ecology of Everyday Life: Rethinking the Desire for Nature* (Montreal: Black Rose, 1999), 32.

125 Ole Moen accurately captures this aspect of Kaczynski's argument: "Kaczynski seeks to initiate a revolutionary movement that will aim to 'kill' technological civilization. This is a good aim for a revolutionary movement, he argues, since it is a simple aim that has a clear criterion for success, and once success is achieved, the revolution will be irreversible. These features, he suggests, will make the anti-tech revolution more likely to succeed than the 20th century socialist revolutions. The socialist revolutionaries had a complicated goal and a vague success criterion. Eradicating technology is more clear-cut. Moreover, since the socialist revolutions only changed the structure of society, the revolutions could be undone. The anti-tech revolution, by contrast, essentially involves the destruction of all advanced technological tools." Moen, "The Unabomber's ethics" *Bioethics* vol. 33 no. 2 (2019), 223-29.

126 Kaczynski, *Technological Slavery*, 171.

3.

Disney Ecology

The Walt Disney movie *Bambi*, one of the best-known films of all time, is more than a treacly children's fable. The tale of Bambi and Thumper is also a parable about habitat destruction, as seen through the eyes of various furry critters. One of the movie's dramatic high points comes in a scene which I still recall vividly from the first time I saw it at age ten. All the animals are grazing peacefully in a meadow at the forest's edge when the soundtrack shifts to ominous tones. Suddenly the creatures scatter in every direction, and after several harrowing moments of chaos and confusion, Bambi finds his way back to his mother. Shaken, he asks her what happened. In a grave voice she responds: *"Man was in the forest."*

This one line, spoken by a cartoon doe and absorbed by generations of children, epitomizes much that is wrongheaded in North American environmentalist thought. "Man was in the forest" signifies, to Bambi and to the audience, that the mere presence of humans in a natural landscape is threatening and dangerous. The message this sends, the ideology it projects, is that human interaction with the natural world is by definition destructive. In much more subtle and sophisticated forms, this same notion animates an alarmingly large proportion of contemporary environmental activists: People as such are bad for animals and ecosystems alike.

Aside from revealing a thoroughly Disneyan contempt for historical and social specificity, this view is ecologically hopeless: the only choice it leaves us is despair. This view means that stemming and reversing the environmental crisis, and undertaking an ecological reconstruction of the devastation that "Man" has wrought, are simply impossible. If humans are per se hazardous to the earth, there is no point in trying to reshape societal structures or change environmental practices; habitat destruction, species loss, and a poisoned planet are inevitable as long as we're around.

Unfortunately, such misguided attitudes often reach their peak in the crucial issue of wilderness defense. Many environmentalists most active and militant in this arena—an immensely important one for the radical ecology movement as a whole—are inclined to portray wilderness as those regions that are untouched by human impact of any sort. In keeping with the patriarchal terminology of "Man's" inexorable destructiveness, the notion of "virgin forests" propagates the false idea that the remaining large tracts of old-growth trees have reached their supposedly pristine state without any human influence, and that the best way to protect such areas is to reduce or eliminate all forms of human contact with them.

This perspective is not just historically naive; it surreptitiously endorses the imperialist view of the North American continent put forth by the European conquerors. For these grand forests that today appear as wilderness were populated for millennia by indigenous peoples who left their mark on the landscape in myriad ways. The symbiotic relationships established between indigenous communities and the woodlands they lived in often enhanced, rather than detracted from, biodiversity. Far from representing some mythical untouched terrain, remaining old-growth forests should properly be seen as the product of particular human influences. (Of course, there are also many historical examples of indigenous practices that had dire environmental effects; the romantic image of native peoples as ecological saints is yet another racist myth.)

If we want to avoid this sort of historical ignorance, radical ecologists need to resist the tempting simplifications of Disney Ecology. In our engagement within environmental movements, in social struggles of various sorts, in interactions with our co-workers and neighbors, we can offer an alternative to the ideology of humans-as-cancer. Social ecology's insistence on the societal roots of environmental disruption, and the vision of social and ecological reconstruction it upholds, point to a fundamentally different way of understanding the ecological crisis and our possible reactions to it. Building on social ecology's insights, radical environmental activists can help create a coherent alternative to Disney Ecology: an ecological humanism.

This won't be a simple task, but it is a vitally important one. Half a century ago, when I first saw *Bambi*, the goal of environmentalists was to convince people of the seriousness, indeed the reality, of the ecological crisis. That struggle has not been definitively won, but it has shifted into a new phase. The challenge we face today is to formulate an appropriate analysis of and response to this crisis—one that is radical, emancipatory, and sustainable. Social ecology offers us the critical tools to help meet that challenge in the years to come.

4.

Ambiguities of Animal Rights

Throughout Europe and North America, a considerable portion of the contemporary radical scene takes for granted the notion that animal liberation is an integral part of revolutionary politics. Many talented and dedicated activists in anti-capitalist and anti-authoritarian movements came to political maturity in the context of animal rights campaigns, and in some circles veganism and animal liberation are considered the apogee of oppositional authenticity.[1]

In order to contest these views, and critically examine the philosophical and political presuppositions that underlie them, it is not necessary to defend or condone the exploitation of non-human animals in factory farms, cosmetics laboratories, and elsewhere. Much of the current industrialized manufacture of animal products is socially worthless and ecologically disastrous, as is to be expected in an economy organized around commodification and profit. Nor does the critique of animal rights entail the wholesale rejection of others' personal convictions or lifestyle choices. There are a number of legitimate reasons to abstain from eating meat or to oppose cruelty to animals.

This essay explores some of the illegitimate reasons for doing so. Such an undertaking is fraught with difficulties, not least of which is the strained sense of incredulity and indignation that critiques of animal rights generally arouse. The topic leads onto tricky terrain, both ethically and politically, in part because it directly impinges on dietary predilections, a matter that is at once profoundly private and inescapably public. Although an animal rights outlook involves much more than vegetarianism or veganism, it does tend to exacerbate the seemingly inherent self-righteousness of food politics, where puritanism is often mistaken for radicalism.[2]

It is nevertheless essential to face such misgivings squarely, in the hope of provoking a more thoughtful debate on the merits of animal rights. I view animal rights thinking as a specific kind of moral mistake and a symptom of political confusion. Much like its ideological cousin, pacifism, the political and moral theory of animal rights offers simple but false answers to important ethical questions. At the risk of collapsing competing versions of animal rights theory into one monolithic category, I would like to consider several of these questions from a social-ecological perspective in order to show why much of the ideology of animal rights is both anti-humanist and anti-ecological, and why its reasoning is frequently at odds with the project of creating a free world.[3]

As an attempt to extend traditional ethical frameworks to non-human nature, animal rights viewpoints are simultaneously much too ambitious and much too timid. They fundamentally misconstrue what is distinctive about humans and our relation to the natural world as well as to the realm of moral action, and at the same time treat "higher" animals anthropomorphically while ignoring the vast majority of creatures that make this planet what it is. But the problem with animal rights thinking goes deeper still. The very project of simply extending existing moral systems, rather than radically transforming them, is flawed from the start.

Many animal rights theorists readily acknowledge that mainstream western traditions of ethical thought are unsatisfactory, but they focus their criticisms on traditional morality's supposed anthropocentrism. This is unconvincing; the primary problem with the mainstream western tradition is not that it promotes anthropocentric ethics, but that it promotes bourgeois ethics, patriarchal ethics, colonial ethics, and so forth.[4] The basic categories of academic moral philosophy are steeped in capitalist values, from the notion of "interests" to the notion of "contract"; the standard analysis of "moral standing" replicates exchange relations, and the individualist conception of "moral agents" obscures the social contexts which produce and sustain agency or hinder it.

Yet these categories are the same ones that animal rights theorists ask us to apply to those creatures (some of them, anyway) that have typically been neglected by moral philosophy. In this way, animal liberation doctrine perpetuates and reinforces the liberal assumptions that are hegemonic within contemporary capitalist cultures, under the guise of contesting these assumptions. Indeed one of the chief reasons for the popularity of animal rights within radical circles is that it appears to offer an extreme affront to the status quo while actually recuperating the ideological foundations of the status quo.

Relying on a dubious analogy to institutionalized forms of social domination and hierarchy, animal rights advocates argue that drawing an ethically significant distinction between human beings and non-human animals is an example of "speciesism," a mere prejudice that illegitimately privileges members of one's own species over members of other species. According to this theory, animals that display a certain level of relative physiological and psychological complexity— usually vertebrates, that is, fish, amphibians, reptiles, birds and mammals—have the same basic moral status as humans. A central nervous system is, at bottom, what confers moral considerability; in some versions of the theory, only creatures with the capacity to experience pain have any moral status whatsoever. These animals are often designated as "sentient."

Thus on the animal rights view, to draw a line between human beings and other sentient creatures is arbitrary and unwarranted, in the same way that classical racism and sexism unjustly deemed women and people of color to be undeserving of moral equality. The next logical step in expanding the circle of ethical concern is to overcome speciesism and grant equal consideration to the interests of all sentient beings, human and non-human.[5]

These arguments are seductive but spurious. The central analogy to the civil rights movement and the women's movement is trivializing and ahistorical. Both of those social movements were initiated and driven by members of the dispossessed and excluded groups themselves, not by benevolent men or white people acting on their behalf. Both movements were built around the idea of reclaiming and reasserting a shared *humanity* in the face of a society that had deprived it and denied it. No civil rights activist or feminist ever argued, "We're sentient beings too!" They argued, "We're fully human too!" Animal liberation doctrine, far from extending this humanist impulse, directly undermines it.

Moreover, the animal rights stance forgets a crucial fact about ethical action. There is indeed a critically important distinction between moral agents (beings who can engage in ethical deliberation, entertain alternative moral choices, and act according to their best judgement) and all other morally considerable beings. Moral agents are uniquely capable of formulating, articulating, and defending a conception of their own interests. No other morally considerable beings are capable of this; in order for their interests to be taken into account in ethical deliberation, these interests must be imputed and interpreted by some moral agent. As far as we know, mentally competent adult human beings are the only moral agents there are.[6]

This decisive distinction is fundamental to ethics itself. To act ethically means, among other things, to respect the principle that persuasion and consent are preferable to coercion and manipulation. This principle cannot be directly applied to human interactions with non-human animals.[7] Animals cannot be persuaded and cannot give consent. In order to accord proper consideration to an animal's well-being, moral agents must make some determination of what that animal's interests are. This is not only unnecessary in the case of other moral agents, it is morally prohibited under normal conditions.

To grasp the significance of this difference, consider the following scenario. I live with several people and a number of cats, toward whom I have various ethical responsibilities. If I am convinced that one of my human housemates needs to take some kind of medicine, it is not acceptable for me to force feed it to her, assuming she is not suffering from psychosis. Instead, I can try to persuade her, through rational deliberation and ethical argument, that it would be best if she took the medicine. But if I think that one of the cats needs to take some kind of medicine, I may well have no choice but to force feed it to him or trick him into eating it.[8] In other words, taking the interests of animals seriously and treating them as morally considerable beings requires a very different sort of ethical action from the sort that is typically appropriate with other people.

The failure to account for this salient feature of moral conduct is one reason why so many proponents of animal rights are hostile to humanist values. But an equally serious failing of animal rights thinking is its obliviousness to ecological values. Recall that on the animal rights view, only individual creatures endowed with sentience deserve moral consideration. Trees, flowers, lakes, rivers, forests, ecosystems, and even most creatures that zoologists classify as "animals" have no interests, well-being, or worth of their own, except inasmuch as they promote the interests of sentient beings. Animal rights advocates have traded in speciesism for phylumism.[9]

Thus even on its own terms, as an attempt to expand the circle of moral consideration beyond the human realm to the natural world, animal rights falls severely short. But the problem is not merely one of inadequate scope. The individual rights approach, with its concomitant view of interests, suffering, and welfare, is difficult to reconcile with an ecological perspective. The well-being of a complex functioning ecological community, with its soils, rocks, waters, micro-organisms, and animal and plant denizens, cannot be reduced to the well-being of those denizens as individuals. The dynamic relationships among the constituent members are as important as the disparate interests of each member of the ensemble.

To focus on the interests of singular animals (and on the small minority of sentient ones at that), and to posit a general duty not to harm these interests or cause suffering, is to miss this ecological dimension entirely.[10] Conflicting interests are part of what accounts for the magnificent variety and complexity of the natural world; the notion of granting equal consideration to all such interests is incoherent in evolutionary as well as ecological terms. This would remain the case even in a completely vegetarian society populated solely by organic subsistence farmers; food cultivation of any sort means the systematic deprivation of habitat and sustenance for some animals and requires the continuous frustration of their interests. Extending the individual rights paradigm to sentient animals simply obscures this fundamental facet of terrestrial existence.[11]

Animal rights thus degrades, rather than develops, the humanist impulse embodied in liberatory social movements, and its basic philosophical thrust is directly contrary to the project of elaborating an ecological ethics. As a moral theory, it leaves much to be desired. But what of its political affiliations and its practical implications? Here as well skepticism is in order.

Nearly all factions in the animal rights camp appear to share a profound faith in the revolutionary potential of purchasing decisions and consumer choices: If enough people stop buying meat, factory farms will go out of business. This commitment to consumer politics is a classically voluntarist approach to social change which further highlights animal liberation's debt to liberalism. It also reveals an elementary misunderstanding of the structure of capitalist economies.[12] Even within the narrow confines of "ethical shopping," however, an animal rights perspective frequently confuses the relevant issues. Instead of investigating the social and ecological conditions under which bananas and coffee reach shopping carts and kitchen tables in Seattle and Stockholm, the myopic focus on sentience asks us to cast a suspicious eye on locally raised free-range poultry.

This regressive shift from the political economy of food production to the pangs of conscience of individual consumption is testimony to the underlying class bias and cultural insularity that run throughout much of the animal rights tendency. Animal rights takes the range of nutritional choices typical of a narrow socio-economic stratum and elevates it to a universal virtue, while stigmatizing sources of protein commonly available to economically deprived urban communities, rural working class families, and peasants in the global south.[13]

The unexamined cultural prejudices embedded deep within animal rights thinking carry political implications that are unavoidably elitist. A consistent animal rights stance, after all, would require many aboriginal peoples to abandon sustainable livelihoods and lifeways completely. Animal rights has no reasonable alternative to offer to longstanding indigenous methods among communities like the Inuit, whose very existence in their ecological niche is predicated on hunting animals. An animal rights viewpoint can only look down disdainfully on peasant societies in Latin America and elsewhere that depend on small-scale animal husbandry as an integral part of their diet, as well as pastoralists in Africa and Asia who rely centrally upon animals to maintain traditional subsistence economies which long predate the colonial imposition of capitalism. These are not matters of "taste" but of sustainability and survival.[14]

Forsaking such practices makes no ecological or social sense, and would be tantamount to eliminating these distinctive societies themselves, all for the sake of assimilation to standards of morality and nutrition propounded by middle-class westerners convinced of their own rectitude. Too many animal rights proponents forget that their belief system is essentially a European-derived construct and neglect the practical repercussions of universalizing it into an unqualified principle of human moral conduct as such.[15]

Nowhere is this combination of parochialism and condescension more apparent than in the animus against hunting. Many animal rights enthusiasts cannot conceive of hunting as anything other than a brutal and senseless activity undertaken for contemptible reasons. Heedless of their own prejudices, they take hunting for an expression of speciesist prejudice. What animal rights theorists malign as "sport hunting" often provides a significant seasonal supplement to the diets of rural populations who lack the luxuries of tempeh and seitan.

Even indigenous communities engaged in conspicuously low-impact traditional hunting have been harassed and vilified by animal rights activists. The campaign against seal hunting in the 1980's, for example, prominently targeted Inuit practices.[16] In the late 1990's, the Makah people of Neah Bay in the northwestern United States tried to re-establish their communal whale hunt, harvesting exactly one gray whale in 1999. The Makah hunt was non-commercial, for subsistence purposes, and fastidiously humane; they chose a whale species that is not endangered and went to considerable lengths to accommodate anti-whaling sentiment.

Nevertheless, when the Makah attempted to embark on their first expedition in 1998, they were physically confronted by the Sea Shepherd Society and other animal protection organizations, who occupied Neah Bay for several months. For these groups, animal rights took precedence over human rights. Many of these animal advocates embellished their pro-whale rhetoric with hoary racist stereotypes about native people and allied themselves with unreconstructed apologists for colonial domination and dispossession.[17]

Such examples are far from rare. Animal rights has frequently served as an entry point for right-wing positions into left movements. Because much of the left has generally been reluctant to think clearly and critically about nature, about biological politics, and about ethical complexity, this unsettling affinity between animal rights and right-wing politics—an affinity which has a lengthy historical pedigree—remains a serious concern. While hardly typical of the current as a whole, it is not unusual to find the most militant proponents of animal liberation also espousing staunch opposition to abortion, homosexuality, and other purportedly "unnatural" phenomena. The "Hardline" tendency, which spread from North America to Europe in the 1990's, is perhaps the most striking example.[18]

But the connections to reactionary politics extend substantially further. The Russian ultranationalist youth group "Moving Together" made animal protection one of the central planks in its platform, while the Swiss "Association Against Animal Factories" wallows in antisemitic propaganda. In Denmark, the first party with a designated portfolio for animal concerns was the anti-immigrant Danish People's Party, and the far-right British National Party boasts of its commitment to animal rights. The contemporary neo-fascist scene in Europe and North America has shown an abiding interest in the theme as well; over the last several decades a range of "National Revolutionaries" and "Third Positionists" have become actively involved in animal rights campaigns.[19]

Although this overlap between animal liberation politics and the xenophobic and authoritarian right may seem incongruous, it has played a prominent role in the history of fascism since the early twentieth century. Various fascist theoreticians prided themselves on their movement's steadfast rejection of anthropocentrism, and German strands of fascism in particular frequently tended toward an animal rights position. Nazi biology textbooks insisted that "there exist no physical or psychological characteristics which would justify a differentiation of mankind from the animal world."[20] Hitler himself was committed to animal welfare causes, and was a vegetarian and opponent of vivisection. His lieutenant Goebbels declared: "The Fuhrer is a convinced vegetarian, on principle. His arguments cannot be refuted on any serious basis. They are totally unanswerable."[21] German vegetarian organizations praised Hitler as the very model of healthy and natural living.[22] Other leading Nazis, like Rudolf Hess, were even stricter in their vegetarianism, and elements in the party promoted raw fruits and nuts as the ideal diet, much like the most scrupulous vegans today. Himmler excoriated hunting and reportedly introduced a vegetarian regimen in the top ranks of the SS, while Goering banned animal experimentation.[23]

The list of pro-animal predilections on the part of top Nazis is long, but more important are the animal rights policies implemented by the Nazi state and the underlying ideology that justified them. Within a few months of taking power, the Nazis passed animal welfare laws that were unprecedented in scale and that explicitly affirmed the moral status of animals independent of any human interest. These decrees stressed the duty to avoid causing pain to animals and established detailed guidelines for interactions with them. According to a leading scholar of Nazi animal legislation, "the Animal Protection Law of 1933 was probably the strictest in the world."[24] Other scholars emphasize the 1933 law's shift from anthropocentric principles to ethical animal protection, putting the wellbeing of animals rather than human sensibilities first. The law was seen at the time as the fulfillment of the German animal rights movement's enduring aims; activists acclaimed it for recognizing that animals are "sentient beings."[25] International animal protection groups celebrated it as well, and Hitler received awards and honors from American, French, Swiss, Swedish and other animal rights organizations.[26]

A 1939 compendium of Nazi animal protection statutes proclaimed that "the German people have always had a great love for animals and have always been conscious of our strong ethical obligations toward them." Nazi laws insisted on "the right which animals inherently possess to be protected in and of themselves."[27] These were not mere philosophical postulates; the ordinances regulated the permissible treatment of domestic and wild animals and designated a variety of protected species while restricting commercial and scientific use of animals. The official reasoning behind these decrees was remarkably similar to latter-day animal rights arguments. "To the German, animals are not merely creatures in the organic sense, but creatures who lead their own lives and who are endowed with perceptive facilities, who feel pain and experience joy," observed Goering in 1933 while announcing a new anti-vivisection law.[28] Nazi supporters of animal rights endorsed these views while condemning "the exaggerated intellectualism of anthropocentric thinkers."[29]

While contemporary animal liberation activists would certainly do well to acquaint themselves with this ominous record of past and present collusion by animal advocates with fascists, the point of reviewing these facts is not to suggest an inevitable connection between animal rights and fascism.[30] But the historical pattern is unmistakable and demands explanation. What helps to account for this consistent intersection of apparently contrary worldviews is a common preoccupation with purity. The presumption that true virtue requires repudiating ostensibly unclean practices such as meat eating furnishes much of the heartfelt vehemence behind animal rights discourse. When disconnected from an articulated critical social perspective and a comprehensive ecological sensibility, this abstentionist version of puritan politics can easily slide into a distorted vision of ethnic, sexual, or ideological purity.

A closely related trope is the recurrent insistence within animal rights thinking on a unitary approach to moral questions. Rightly rejecting the inherited dualism of humanity and non-human nature, animal rights philosophers wrongly collapse the two into one undifferentiated whole, thus substituting monism for dualism (and neglecting most of the natural world in the process). But regressive dreams of purity and oneness carry no emancipatory potential; their political ramifications range from trite to dangerous. In the wrong hands, a simplistic critique of "speciesism" yields liberation for neither people nor animals, but merely the same hapless anti-humanism that has always turned radical hopes into their reactionary opposite.

Rather than positing a static, one-dimensional moral landscape populated by humans and animals facing one another on equal terms, those drawn to animal rights might consider a more complex alternative: an integrated ethical viewpoint that encompasses a social dimension and an ecological dimension without conflating the two. Such an approach recognizes the crucial continuity between humankind and the rest of the natural world while respecting the ethically significant distinctions that mark this continuum. Incorporating a dialectical view of natural processes and entities, this alternative perspective comprehends the breathtaking abundance, sophistication, and diversity of life forms and living communities on the earth as an occasion for awe and as valuable in themselves.

The evolutionary dynamic that generated this wondrous profusion of life can be understood as a dialectic of cooperation and competition.[31] Humans are the first creatures capable of transcending this dialectic, which gave rise to us, by consciously advancing the moment of cooperation—that is, by structuring our interactions with each other and with other creatures along mutually beneficial lines. This cooperative potential has two distinct components: one interhuman and social, and the other interspecific and ecological.[32]

Within the social sphere, the potential for cooperative relations is, in an important sense, universal. While it would be naïve to suppose that contradictory interests will disappear in a free society, there is no 'natural' reason for the persistence of large-scale social competition. In regard to the rest of the biosphere, on the other hand, this cooperative potential is notably circumscribed. It is not just impossible to eliminate competition among organisms over resources, habitats, and so forth; the very notion is profoundly incompatible with the basic parameters of living systems. The potentials for cooperation between humans and other animals are thus more modest and more particular.

An ecologically and socially credible effort to take animal interests seriously will dispense with the notion that killing and harm are wrong per se, and will surmount the dichotomy of sentient versus non-sentient beings by integrating a concern for animal welfare into an inclusive appreciation for the well-being of whole ecological communities.[33] In practice, this would likely result in a revival and refinement of the custom of humane treatment of animals, accompanied by the insight that cultivating humanist values is a component of, rather than a hindrance to, this endeavor. People will not consistently treat animals humanely until people—all people—are treated humanely.

None of these ethical potentialities can be realized, however, as long as we continue to replicate social institutions built around domination and hierarchy. Overcoming those structures will require a revolutionary transformation, ethically as well as politically. This momentous historical goal can only be reached by a movement that reclaims, not rejects, the uniquely human capacity for freedom. In their present form, the philosophy and politics of animal rights cannot guide us toward this goal.

Notes

1   For purposes of this essay, I am ignoring the differences between "animal rights" and "animal liberation" discourses. I will use both terms more or less interchangeably to designate the belief that harming and killing non-human animals is on the whole morally impermissible. Since I can no longer do so in person, I would like to express my profound gratitude to feminist philosopher Claudia Card, who passed away in 2015. As a teacher and writer, as an intellectual innovator and personal pioneer, Claudia was a model of engaged ethical thinking. From an early stage she challenged and supported my work in a critical dialogue extending over two decades. She disagreed firmly with several of the arguments I develop here, but her example shaped my approach to ethical and ecological questions in lasting ways.

2   A further complication stems from the fact that many advocates of animal rights are also determined practitioners of an elusive eclecticism: When challenged on philosophical grounds, they quickly shift the terms of the dispute onto political territory. When their political claims are rebutted, they fall back on arguments about economics or religion or biology or personal health, cutting a broad swath through anthropology, linguistics, psychology, and a host of other fields. This can make it difficult to assess what is at stake and why. I will try to take account of a variety of animal rights positions in my critique.

3   My discussion is primarily based on the following texts: Peter Singer, *Animal Liberation* (New York: Harper, 2002); Tom Regan, *The Case for Animal Rights* (London: Routledge, 1988); Mary Midgley, *Animals and Why They Matter* (Athens: University of Georgia Press, 1998); James Rachels, *Created from Animals: The*

Moral Implications of Darwinism (Oxford: Oxford University Press, 1999); David DeGrazia, *Taking Animals Seriously* (Cambridge: Cambridge University Press, 2001); Gary Francione, *Rain Without Thunder: The Ideology of the Animal Rights Movement* (Philadelphia: Temple University Press, 1996).

4   Anthropocentrism is an ideology that serves to mask the crucial divisions within humankind. Animal liberationists are not alone in misapprehending the function of anthropocentrism; this misunderstanding is widely dispersed throughout contemporary environmental philosophy. Social change movements often err by mistaking entrenched institutions for mere ideologies (consider, for example, critiques of racism that conceive of it as a collection of attitudes to be changed by appeals to conscience); this is the typical idealism of would-be reformers. The animal rights movement, along with much of ecocentric philosophy, has made the opposite error and thus succumbed to a different sort of idealism. It mistakes the ideology of anthropocentrism for an actual institution, an embodiment of social practice. But there are no powerful anthropocentric institutions, only elitist ones hiding behind a universal veneer. Capitalism, patriarchy, and white supremacy, to choose three prominent examples, do not privilege humans as such, but rather some humans over other humans.

5   The locus classicus for this line of reasoning is Peter Singer's book *Animal Liberation*, which is built around the idea that the social liberation movements of the 1960's led naturally to the animal liberation movement and that the logical structure of racism, sexism and "speciesism" are identical. This thesis, which remains widely influential among animal rights supporters, is belied by the historical record. Even early forms of animal welfare sentiment often took the very opposite trajectory and went hand in hand

with class bias and racial prejudice. For examples see Keith Thomas, *Man and the Natural World* (Oxford: Oxford University Press, 1996), 185-88. Thomas notes that in early modern Britain "it was common to champion animals by comparing them unfavourably with those inferior races of mankind" whose image preoccupied European sensibilities, while opponents of animal cruelty "regularly portrayed dogs and horses as morally superior to natives and savages" (187).

6   Animal rights theorists like to respond that human infants and mentally disabled adults are not agents in this sense, a point which I take to be obvious and irrelevant to the question at hand. I am not arguing that moral considerability is restricted to moral agents, nor that there is a firm ontological divide between humans and other organisms. What the peculiar role of moral agents demonstrates is that some distinctions between different types of moral considerability are very much warranted, and that the mere equal consideration of interests fails to capture several fundamental facets of ethical action.

7   For a searching reflection on human-animal relations that sometimes reaches conclusions different from mine, see Dominick LaCapra, "Reopening the Question of the Human and the Animal" in Lacapra, *History and its Limits: Human, Animal, Violence* (Ithaca: Cornell University Press, 2009), 149-89. As Lacapra argues elsewhere, "the questioning of a radical divide between the human and other animals" is "an ethical and political issue whose problematic nature requires an attempt to come to terms with a complex network of similarities and differences linking humans and other animals with different modes of being." Dominick LaCapra, *Understanding Others: Peoples, Animals, Pasts* (Ithaca: Cornell University Press, 2018), 113-14.

8   To recognize the special status of competent adult humans in this sense is not an instance of privilege or prejudice. It is no more arbitrary than acknowledging that women have a special status in reproductive decisions, that goalkeepers have a special status in soccer games, or that pilots have a special status in aerial transport. To cry "privilege" in this context is analogous to condemning the "injustice" inherent in the fact that only speakers of Hungarian may participate in a conversation in that language. Since cross-species "translation" of this sort is currently impossible, the anomalous position of human moral agents is likely to persist until we encounter other beings capable of engaging in ethical discourse.

9   Technically the phylum Chordata includes animals that have a central nervous system regardless of whether they have a fully formed spinal column; it is the closest taxonomic approximation to the sort of animals that animal rights theorists consider "animals," although many animal rights proponents focus primarily on the even smaller class of mammals. While prominent spokespeople for animal liberation like Peter Singer have explicitly defended the view that no other organisms have any kind of moral standing, this position is not shared by all animal rights philosophers. Tom Regan, for example, acknowledges that non-sentient life forms may have inherent value which could be accounted for within a broader environmental ethic. But a rights framework is patently unsuited to such a project; an equitable ecological ethics cannot be based on the interests of individual organisms, whether sentient or not.

10   The emphasis on suffering is questionable in any case. That physical comfort involves an aversion to pain is a truism, but this tells us little about its moral significance. Especially in its utilitarian variants, animal liberation unproblematically

treats pain as a moral bad and pleasure as a moral good. Such a straightforward identification is implausibly simplistic even within the social realm; there are not a few instances in which pain can be a moral desideratum, as well as cases in which pleasure should be discouraged rather than fostered. The ethical import of sense experiences is entirely context-dependent.

11 The conception of rights as individual attributes that function as a sort of moral trump evolved in conjunction with the reciprocal notion of responsibilities; each was held to entail the other. These ideas were moreover developed in a social context that emphasized democratic deliberation and the contestation of competing claims, in the course of which rights-bearers continually refined and modified their moral claims. This context cannot be transferred to human-animal interactions. There is no meaningful sense in which non-human animals can be expected to attend to their responsibilities; and their claims to rights can only be advanced representationally, via human intermediaries. Trapped as they are within a liberal conceptual framework, animal rights standpoints are inevitably paternalistic.

12 That production, not circulation, is the decisive sector in market economies has been a mainstay of radical analyses of capitalism since the first volume of *Capital* was published in 1867. But this insight is hardly unique to Marxists. Even mainstream economists concur that consumer spending "is not a driving force in our economy, but a driven one." Robert Heilbroner and Lester Thurow, *Economics Explained* (New York: Simon & Schuster, 1998), 92. For historical examples of the ways in which a focus on individual consumption can detract from a radical political vision see Finis Dunaway, *Seeing Green: The Use and Abuse of American Environmental Images* (Chicago: University of Chicago Press,

2015); Laura Miller, *Building Nature's Market: The Business and Politics of Natural Foods* (Chicago: University of Chicago Press, 2017); Maria McGrath, *Food for Dissent: Natural Foods and the Consumer Counterculture since the 1960s* (Amherst: University of Massachusetts Press, 2019).

13 Kathryn Paxton George's book *Animal, Vegetable, or Woman? A Feminist Critique of Ethical Vegetarianism* (Albany: State University of New York Press, 2000) provocatively criticizes this elitist cultural and physiological model, along with its curiously myopic nutritional assumptions, as an expression of masculine bias. In a similar vein, Michael Pollan's 2002 article "An Animal's Place" diagnoses animal rights as a quintessentially urban ideology that reflects a detached and distorted relationship with the natural world. (Pollan's article can be found at http://michaelpollan.com/articles-archive/an-animals-place/)

14 This point bears emphasizing because it reveals one of the most consistently problematic aspects of conventional animal rights thinking. Many peasant societies in widely different parts of the world incorporate various forms of small-scale animal agriculture, and some indigenous cultures feature diets based primarily on animals. It is hard to see why it would be either socially or ecologically better for those food systems to abjure reliance on animals and animal products.

15 It is certainly true that many non-western cultural traditions have cultivated a markedly more respectful attitude toward animals, and many Europeans and Euro-Americans have come to vegetarianism through an encounter with Eastern spiritual traditions, usually refracted through an orientalist and Romantic lens. My point is simply that the full-fledged philosophy of animal rights is ultimately a reaction against the western heritage's

comparative lack of attention to animals—a reaction which itself stands well within the boundaries of that heritage.

16 On the anti-sealing campaign and its impact on Inuit society see George Wenzel, *Animal Rights, Human Rights: Ecology, Economy and Ideology in the Canadian Arctic* (Toronto: University of Toronto Press, 1991).

17 For an incisive early analysis of the Makah whaling conflict see Alx Dark's article "The Makah Whale Hunt" (available at http://www.cnie.org/nae/cases/makah/). Subsequent treatments include Rob van Ginkel, "The Makah Whale Hunt and Leviathan's Death: Reinventing Tradition and Disputing Authenticity in the Age of Modernity" *Etnofoor* 17 (2004), 58-89; Michael Marker, "After the Makah Whale Hunt: Indigenous Knowledge and Limits to Multicultural Discourse" *Urban Education* 41 (2006), 482-505; and the chapter on the Makah whaling controversy in Claire Jean Kim, *Dangerous Crossings: Race, Species, and Nature in a Multicultural Age* (Cambridge: Cambridge University Press, 2015).

18 The "Hardline" faction grew out of the Straight Edge movement in punk culture, combining uncompromising veganism with purportedly "pro-life" politics. Hardliners believe in self-purification from various forms of "pollution": animal products, tobacco, alcohol, drugs, and "deviant" sexual behavior, including abortion, homosexuality, and indeed any sex for pleasure rather than procreation. Their version of animal liberation professes absolute authority based on the "laws of nature." The "Hardline Creed" reads in part: "The time has come for an ideology and for a movement that is both physically and morally strong enough to do battle against the forces of evil that are destroying the earth (and all life upon it). [...] That ideology, that movement, is Hardline. A belief system, and a way of life that lives by one ethos—that

all innocent life is sacred, and must have the right to live out its
natural state of existence in peace, without interference. [...] Any
action that does interfere with such rights shall not be considered
a "right" in itself, and therefore shall not be tolerated. Those who
hurt or destroy life around them, or create a situation in which that
life or the quality of it is threatened shall from then on no longer
be considered innocent life, and in turn will no longer have rights.
Adherents to the hardline will abide by these principles in daily
life. They shall live at one with the laws of nature, and shall not
forsake them for the desire of pleasure—from deviant sexual acts
and/or abortion, to drug use of any kind (and all other cases where
one harms all life around them under the pretext that they are just
harming themselves). And, in following with the belief that one
shall not infringe on an innocent's life—no animal product shall
be consumed (be it flesh, milk or egg). Along with this purity of
everyday life, the true hardliner must strive to liberate the rest of
the world from its chains—saving lives in some cases, and in others,
dealing out justice to those guilty of destroying it." More recent
variations on these ideas can be found at the "Vegan Final Solution"
website (motto: "the final solution for vegan revolution").

19 The National Revolutionary and Third Position currents trace
their lineage back to leading fascists from the 1920's and 1930's,
especially to "dissident" Nazis like the Strasser brothers. The
flirtation between neo-fascists and animal liberationists is
neither new nor a one-sided affair. A quarter of a century ago
Jutta Ditfurth provided an excellent overview of the upsurge in
extreme right views among animal rights groups in Germany
in her book *Entspannt in die Barbarei* (Hamburg: Konkret,
1996), especially chapter 5. For a more recent critical account
see Mira Landwehr, *"Vier Beine gut, zwei Beine schlecht": Zum*

Zusammenhang von Tierliebe und Menschenhass in der veganen Tierrechtsbewegung (Hamburg: Konkret, 2019); for a conservative British view see "Neo-nazis join animal rights groups" *The Telegraph* September 3, 2000; for a Swedish perspective see Heléne Lööw, "The Idea of Purity: The Swedish Racist Counterculture, Animal Rights, and Environmental Protection" in Jeffrey Kaplan, ed., *The Cultic Milieu: Oppositional Subcultures in an Age of Globalization* (Lanham: Rowman & Littlefield, 2002), 193-210. A broad-based study of the European far right argues that support for animal rights sometimes forms a notable element of contemporary far right ideology and practice, based on opposition to anthropocentrism and an emphasis on animal sentience; see Kristian Voss, "Nature and Nation in Harmony: The Ecological Component of Far Right Ideology" (dissertation, European University Institute, 2014), 120-28. Voss concludes that "the anti-anthropocentrism of the far right especially manifests itself as a passionate defense of animals as sentient beings" (261).

20 Quoted in Louis Snyder, *Encyclopedia of the Third Reich* (London: Hale, 1998), 79. This stance had a long history within right-wing circles in Germany in the late nineteenth and early twentieth centuries, a period when vegetarianism and animal welfare sentiment often went hand in hand with racial mythology and authoritarian political and cultural beliefs.

21 Joseph Goebbels quoted in Robert Proctor, *The Nazi War on Cancer* (Princeton: Princeton University Press, 1999), 136. Chapter 5 of Proctor's book, "The Nazi Diet," offers an informed assessment of Nazism's food politics.

22 See e.g. *Neuleben: Zeitschrift für natürliche Lebensgestaltung* March 1935, 59-60; the periodical was the official "Mitteilungsblatt des Verbandes deutscher Vegetarier-Vereine." Additional examples can

be found in Joachim Scholz, *"Haben wir die Jugend, so haben wir die Zukunft": Die Obstbausiedlung Eden als alternatives Gesellschafts- und Erziehungsmodell, 1893-1936* (Berlin: Weidler, 2002), 31-33, and Ulrike Thoms, "Vegetarianism, Meat and Life Reform in Early Twentieth-Century Germany and their Fate in the 'Third Reich'" in David Cantor, ed., *Meat, Medicine and Human Health in the Twentieth Century* (London: Routledge, 2016), 145-57. Thoms provides a nuanced portrait of vegetarian movements in the Nazi era. For discussion of Hitler's vegetarian habits see Ian Kershaw, *Hitler 1889-1936: Hubris* (New York: Norton, 1999), 345 and 703; Kershaw tentatively concludes that Hitler came to embrace "complete vegetarianism." On Mussolini's support for animal protection see chapter II in Giulia Guazzaloca, *Primo: non maltrattare. Storia della protezione degli animali in Italia* (Rome: Laterza, 2018).

23 Compare Jost Hermand, *Grüne Utopien in Deutschland* (Frankfurt: Fischer, 1991), 114; Boria Sax, *Animals in the Third Reich* (New York: Continuum, 2000), 35; Thoms, "Vegetarianism, Meat and Life Reform," 154-55.

24 Sax, *Animals in the Third Reich*, 112. Sax's book is an invaluable source on Nazi attitudes toward animals.

25 Ludwig Zukowsky, "Der deutsche Tierschutz—ein Werk des Führers!" *Reichstierschutzblatt* May 1939, 1-2.

26 Stefan Dirscherl, *Tier- und Naturschutz im Nationalsozialismus: Gesetzgebung, Ideologie und Praxis* (Göttingen: Vandenhoeck & Ruprecht, 2012), 48, 79, 158-59.

27 Quoted in Luc Ferry, *The New Ecological Order* (Chicago: University of Chicago Press, 1995), 99-100. Sax gives a compact exposition of the same passage in *Animals in the Third Reich*, 121-22.

28 Hermann Goering quoted in Sax, *Animals in the Third Reich*, 111. For readers familiar with the philosophical literature on animal

liberation, it is impossible to miss the resonances in this passage
with Regan's conception of sentient animals as "subjects of a life"
and Singer's emphasis on their capacity for experiencing pain. The
legacy of Nazi animal rights measures ought to be reason enough
(if any more were needed) for animal liberation proponents to
abandon their ill-considered comparisons between factory farms
and the death camps.

29 Eduard Tratz, *Natur ist alles* (Berlin: Ahnenerbe-Stiftung, 1943), 29.

30 In fact a number of left advocates of animal rights are also active
anti-fascists. My critique is not meant to impugn their political
commitment but to draw attention to the philosophical and
historical ambiguities involved in the attempt to combine social
emancipation with animal liberation.

31 This insight is anything but new; in its modern form it extends at
least back to Kropotkin. Animal rights enthusiasts seem alternately
to forget the competitive and the cooperative aspects of this
process, and above all appear to ignore the fact that all creatures
are eventually food for other creatures—a fate that is entirely fitting
and not the least bit troubling. This is not nature red in tooth and
claw, but the incomparable beauty of natural evolution.

32 This position aligns in several ways with the "partnership ethic"
outlined by Carolyn Merchant, based on "a partnership between
nonhuman nature and the human community." See Merchant,
Reinventing Eden: The Fate of Nature in Western Culture (New
York: Routledge, 2013), 191-97. Likewise, my argument bears
important similarities to the "ethic of flourishing" developed by
Chris Cuomo in *Feminism and ecological communities: An ethic of
flourishing* (New York: Routledge, 1998); see 42-43 and 93-105 for
her discerning discussion of animal rights.

33 In the years since this essay was originally published, it has

generated a series of thoughtful critical responses from exponents of more complex and politically perceptive varieties of animal rights; for a recent example see Dayton Martindale, "The Social Ecological Case for Animal Liberation: Towards an Interspecies Communalism" in the Winter 2019 issue of *Harbinger: A Journal of Social Ecology*. Some of these responses reveal significant common ground that can help bridge contrary positions on animal rights philosophy. Primarily plant-based diets, for instance, can be a good idea for all sorts of reasons that have nothing to do with animal rights, while the abolition of industrial farming can make ecological and social sense regardless of what is being farmed, whether animals or plants. Despite these areas of potential agreement, however, several crucial disagreements remain. One of the most important centers on the invidious criterion of sentience, which I find fundamentally misguided in ethical as well as ecological terms. This criterion is in turn closely related to the individualist assumptions that underlie so much of contemporary animal rights thinking. What I propose instead is an inclusive ecological ethics in tandem with an emancipatory social ethics. On ecological grounds, Lake Superior deserves greater ethical consideration than any individual creature living in it, animal or otherwise, despite the fact that the lake itself lacks all of the elements of moral standing that animal rights frameworks typically identify. In this and other ways, many predominant forms of animal rights and animal liberation are much closer to an anthropocentric position than their proponents realize. By excluding most living beings, not to mention entities like Lake Superior, and fixating on the subjective experience of suffering, they fall far short of both a meaningful ecological ethic and a viable project for radical social change.

5.

Blood and Soil Revived?

Ecological Politics on the Far Right

In August 2019 a white supremacist in Texas killed twenty-three people in the name of protecting the natural world. It was the second such mass murder that year, following a similar anti-immigrant attack in New Zealand five months earlier. The perpetrator in El Paso claimed to be "defending my country" from a "Hispanic invasion." His manifesto mingled opposition to "race mixing" with worries about pollution, consumer waste, and urban sprawl. Anxieties regarding population were a central factor in his muddled rationale. In his own words, he undertook his gruesome actions in order to halt "the decimation of the environment." His stated reasoning was: "If we can get rid of enough people, then our way of life can become more sustainable."[1]

At times of social crisis, the politics of ecology can become not just a subject of ideological debate but a matter of life and death. Naïve beliefs about nature, which are just as common among Greens, progressives, New Agers, and the like, take on a harder edge at the right end of the spectrum. Combined with reactionary doctrines of natural order and a xenophobic resentment of immigrants, they carry significant appeal for a wide swath of the right, from conservatives and authoritarians to neo-Nazi militants and mass murderers. Alongside sensationalist manifestations in fascist paraphernalia and hate crimes, less virulent forms of the same ideology can be found in mainstream circles.

This unfortunate political combination has an extensive history in North America, Europe, and beyond. Its more extreme forms posit an integral connection between natural purity and racial purity, reviving a legacy that seemed to belong to a discredited past. When white supremacists chanted "blood and soil" while marching through the streets of Charlottesville in August 2017, they heralded a renewal of Nazi rhetoric in an unexpected and unsettling context. Primarily associated with the Third Reich, the phrase "blood and soil" predates the Nazi era and has been used in a variety of settings to assert a special bond between a people and their territory.[2] It is often adopted for racist purposes, suggesting a primeval kinship with the landscape, and its recent reappearance is a sign of the environmental ambitions of an emboldened radical right.

Because blood and soil theories do not always come packaged under that label, understanding the resurgence of far right ecological politics in the twenty-first century requires a differentiated approach. Misgivings about population, immigration, and environmental deterioration are not unique to the far right, and their expression varies by country and time period. Charting these permutations across geographical borders and chronological eras yields a complex international portrait that interweaves history and the present day. The following incomplete account can serve as an initial overview to spur further research.

Odious incidents like the El Paso attack are not solitary episodes or simply products of deviance. The implicit blood and soil premises in mainstream thought are closer in motive to such drastic acts than some might want to admit. In the contemporary United States, the underlying beliefs have made substantial inroads within much of the policy establishment. The far-ranging influence of the late John Tanton is a striking example of the durable links between environmental commitment and aggressive anti-immigrant politics.

Until his death in 2019, Tanton was "the leader of the immigration restriction forces among environmentalists" in the US.[3] He was prominently involved in the Sierra Club, the League of Conservation Voters, the Nature Conservancy, and other mainstream environmental groups over the course of decades. Through a series of organizations with innocuous names like the Center for Immigration Studies and the Federation for American Immigration Reform, Tanton oversaw a network of nativists and population control activists that brought conservationists together with hard-core eugenicists.[4] Tanton worked to make white supremacist positions palatable by coupling them with environmental goals. His mentor, Garrett Hardin, was a lifelong proponent of eugenics whose ideas shaped ecological thinking across generations. Both Tanton and Hardin played "a crucial role in anti-immigrant alliance building, fostering relationships among conservationists, green followers of Darwin and Malthus, and the American far right."[5]

Hardin and Tanton have many admirers, and their views are rooted firmly in the American environmental movement's past. Fears of racial degeneration were a driving force among many of the founding figures of American conservationism, who combined wilderness preservation with eugenics, scientific racism, and immigration restriction.[6] In Britain as well, the history of political ecology is entwined with the far right. From the 1930s on, major protagonists in the emergence of organic farming and other environmental practices supported blood and soil views, sometimes in openly fascist form. Their impact was felt in the 1946 establishment of the Soil Association, an essential early platform for organic agriculture in the UK. Several of the founding members of the Soil Association came from a blood and soil background, including Rolf Gardiner, Gerard Wallop, and Jorian Jenks.

Gardiner's enthusiastic pro-Nazi statements in the 1930s lauded Hitler's regime for its "resuscitation of yeoman, peasant values as opposed to industrial, urban, manufacturing values."[7] After the war he continued to correspond with Nazi supporters of organic farming such as Richard Walther Darré, Hermann Reischle, and Alwin Seifert. His colleague Wallop, known as Viscount Lymington and later Lord Portsmouth, celebrated "blood and soil" as early as 1932. He founded the English Array, a pro-fascist back to the land group, in 1936.[8] Jenks was Agricultural Advisor to the British Union of Fascists from 1937 until his imprisonment as an Axis sympathizer in 1940. He edited the journal of the Soil Association, *Mother*

Earth, from its inception in 1946 until his death in 1963. His work is still published by British fascists today, who praise him as "a pioneer of radical ecology and organic farming" and "one of the principal architects of the Green Movement in Britain."[9]

Later generations have continued the legacy of green trends on the far right in the UK, from traditional stalwarts like the British National Party to neo-fascist militants like Troy Southgate. At the height of its popularity in 2010, the BNP declared itself "the only true green party" in Britain, condemning the "grave peril" of immigration as the "number one threat" to nature.[10] Southgate's ideological itinerary has brought him to emphatic support of "ecological issues, anti-capitalism and animal welfare" as part of a "national revolution."[11] Previously a leader in the "Third Position" current, Southgate has long sought to appropriate left themes for the radical right. He advocates "the establishment of decentralised village-communities" and "the revival of rural crafts," with healthy Britons "growing their own food in gardens and allotments or setting up co-operatives" while "bartering and working with alternative currencies through local exchange trading systems." Heartily recommending E.F. Schumacher's *Small is Beautiful* as a key component of his racialist vision, Southgate blames "technological advancement" for the "destruction of the environment."[12]

These developments are not exceptional or unprecedented. In March 1989 the front cover of the British anti-fascist magazine *Searchlight* warned against "The Greening of the Brownshirts."[13] Nor are they peculiar to the anglophone world. In France, as a recent historical study points out, "the origins of organic farming do not lie with the radical left, but instead with the fascist right." Even after 1945, appeals to purity and anxieties about racial decline merged with antisemitic animus and nostalgic idealization of French rural landscapes. "Many of the earliest proponents of organic agriculture had ties to the fascist politics of Vichy and the eugenics movement."[14] The major far right party in France today, Marine Le Pen's National Rally (formerly the National Front), has made environmental concerns central to its close-the-borders demagoguery.[15] Its green orientation is not new; in 1993 the National Front announced that it "believes deeply in the values of ecology," vowing to act as "defender of nature and the natural order."[16]

Ecological questions have been a familiar theme on the Italian extreme right since the 1970s. Current neo-fascist groups like Casa Pound promote "nativist ecology" and denounce immigration as a threat to "biodiversity."[17] Casa Pound has adopted an array of environmental and animal rights stances, "ranging from opposition to the 'industry of the meat' to resistance against the practices of vivisection and the use of animals in circus performances."[18] Austria's principal far right party takes an anti-anthropocentric position in its defense of animals, proclaiming that "animals are not commodities, but sentient beings."[19] The party opposes factory farming and genetically modified organisms while supporting a nuclear free Europe and local organic agriculture.[20]

There is a particularly robust record of anti-immigrant environmentalism on the Swiss far right, where harangues about "overpopulation" as an ecological catastrophe "drew upon classical racism" from the 1960s onward.[21] In Sweden and Norway, the neo-Nazi Nordic Resistance Movement campaigns for animal rights and environmental protection while ranting against Jews and migrants. Its declared aim is "living in harmony with the laws of nature."[22] Since 2007 the chief fascist organization in Greece, the Golden Dawn, has showcased its own "Green Wing" to bolster "ecological consciousness" and publicize "racial and environmental issues." Against "the leftists and the hippies" who tried "to claim the ecologist movement as their own," the Green Wing "educates the People on the dangers of modern life (Monsanto, the energy crisis, forests, plants and animals on the edge of extinction etc.)."[23]

In Russia, the "Ringing Cedars" movement combines back-to-nature ideals and New Age creeds with ethnic nationalism. Also known as the "Anastasia" movement, it has adherents across Eastern Europe, Scandinavia, and elsewhere, with a primary focus on establishing environmentally conscious rural settlements or eco-villages.[24] According to German supporters, these spiritual homesteads will "heal the earth" and reclaim "Lebensraum."[25] While the more benign facets of the movement emphasize eco-communities, vegetarianism, and neo-pagan nature religion, there is a significant far right undercurrent with antisemitic elements. The founding texts of the movement recount an elaborate conspiracy, lasting millennia, led by a High Priest against the "Vedic" culture of ancient Russia, in which the "Jewish people" were "programmed" to "take control of the whole world."[26]

Such examples recall the long history of entanglement between reactionary ideologies and nature mysticism. Neo-pagan and esoteric beliefs are solidly ensconced on the European far right.[27] Eccentric figures like John

Michell and the "Earth Mysteries" movement exemplified the convergence of esotericism and neo-paganism with environmental romanticism in recent decades.[28] But the connections between alternative spirituality and right-wing ecology extend back more than a century and are becoming increasingly prominent in the contemporary far right scene, where environmental as well as spiritual perspectives seem to be rapidly proliferating. Germanic and Nordic forms of these worldviews are especially susceptible to blood and soil themes, rendering "the varieties of nature spirituality that promote a return to 'indigenous' mythic traditions more vulnerable to racial thought."[29] North American enthusiasts of this tradition include now-defunct groups like the White Order of Thule, whose members claimed that "The ecological movement is a white movement, founded by Aryans."[30] They favored an "alliance between radical racism and environmentalism" based on "militant racist biocentrism."[31] Views like these continue to find defenders today.[32]

Invocations of a mythic past, pagan or otherwise, are a common feature in contemporary back to the land efforts on the right. The current revival of the "Artamanen" movement in Germany shows that such ventures are more than just talk. It was the original Artamanen in the 1920s who helped popularize the phrase "blood and soil" as the title of their monthly periodical. Motivated by a combination of anti-urban sentiment and ethnic revanchism, small bands of young Germans embarked on rural projects in the country's eastern borderlands in order to displace Polish agricultural workers and secure "Lebensraum" for the German nation years before Hitler came to power.[33] Heinrich Himmler and other Nazi leaders were early members. Calling for a return to "sacred mother earth," the Artamanen pioneered a racialized vision of agrarian renewal. They were part of a broader trend of *völkisch* ruralism that embraced vegetarianism, anti-industrial romanticism, and nature protection a century ago.[34]

Their would-be successors in the twenty-first century have reclaimed the name "Artamanen" for themselves and put blood and soil principles into practice by founding far right settlements in rural areas of eastern Germany. In their own words, they are "fulfilling the dream of living on the land in harmony with nature."[35] Through villages across the region, the revived Artamanen market right-wing extremism as an environmental lifestyle, growing organic vegetables and selling homemade eco-products to support their projects.[36] In some cases they work together with cadres from the NPD, the leading neo-Nazi party in Germany today, which has its own longstanding history of engagement with ecological issues.[37] Artamanen and NPD members also promote environmental lifestyles via a far right glossy magazine on ecology and health. Billing itself as "the magazine for holistic thinking," it touts green living and animal rights in tandem with Germanic runes, Nordic mythology, and conspiracy lore while praising Nazi measures to protect the natural world.[38] In response to this wave of blood and soil revivalism, German civil society organizations—along with scholars, activists, and journalists—have mounted an impressive campaign of public education, widely disseminating critical analyses of radical right environmental tactics.[39]

Part of that task involves uncovering historical continuities that link multiple generations of environmental dedication with reactionary politics. In Germany as in other societies, these connections can be traced to the nineteenth century. The career of antisemitic agitator Paul Förster offers an illuminating example. A politician for several right-wing parties from the 1880s onward, he called for "the elimination of the Jews from the German nation." He was an enthusiast for various *völkisch* causes and belonged to the Pan-German League. Before and after the turn of the century Förster was a driving force in German antisemitic circles, infamous for his invective against Jews. At the same time he was a passionate advocate for vegetarianism, natural healing, and other "life reform" tenets and held leading positions in international animal protection organizations. He published numerous tracts in defense of animals and used the term "animal rights" a hundred years before it became popular. Förster was also an early critic of vaccination and a proponent of simple living, all under the motto of "back to nature."[40]

Other environmental dignitaries followed a similar trajectory. Some of the foremost conservationists in twentieth century Germany eagerly supported the Nazi regime and then went on to shape the nature protection movement after 1945. Walther Schoenichen, Hans Schwenkel, Heinrich Wiepking, Hans Klose, and Alwin Seifert all held prominent environmental posts in the Third Reich. Far from being scorned by their conservationist colleagues after the defeat of Nazism, they were celebrated as ecological trailblazers. The historical amnesia of German environmentalists in the post-war years, which had a lasting impact on the development of green politics, has been forcefully challenged by a younger generation of scholars.[41] Their efforts have met with remarkable resistance from those who remain reluctant to face this history.[42] Even today, some still fall for the self-exculpatory myths put forward by former Nazis.

Whether past or present, these tendencies are not distinctively German and are by no means limited to Nazis. Right-wing versions of ecological politics can be found around the world.[43] Though they share common themes, there is no overarching belief system that unites them all. Bitter internal controversies are a hallmark of the extreme right, and environmental questions are no different. The range of responses to climate change is a telling case in point; forms of denial that are prevalent among conventional conservatives also attract followers on the far right.[44] Skepticism toward green proposals is customary across many sectors of the right, from populist to nationalist to authoritarian, distorted by traditional ambivalence regarding capitalism and the state. It is easy to view those trends as exclusively anti-environmentalist, rather than as variations on environmental values cast within a right-wing framework. That is a mistake. By failing to recognize that a formidable segment of the far right is "genuinely committed to ecology and the natural world," this approach "prevents us from accurately reading the rapidly changing political landscape."[45]

Within that changing landscape, several elements of right-wing ecology have endured. Race has been a persistent obsession from the beginning, whether expressed as ethnic nationalism or as a primordial racial identity that transcends national borders. The ambiguities of the term "blood and soil" allow a range of interpretations. While the phrase itself is roughly a century old, its European champions routinely claim an ancient pedigree, tracing their roots in the land back to ostensibly autochthonous origins.[46] Their North American counterparts face a more challenging task in asserting a racial connection to the territories they inhabit; in the US such claims are generally based on a sense of "entitlement to stolen Native land."[47] The resulting inconsistencies are perhaps most visible in the domain of the so-called alt-right, whose adherents "fuse deep ecology with explicit white supremacy."[48]

A 2017 statement titled "The Alt-Right is Green" outlines the logic invoked by aspiring defenders of racial and ecological purity. In the contemporary alt-right mindset, "conserving the environment goes hand-in-hand with conserving the White race." Since "Europe and North America are white man's land" whose natural splendor is threatened by contamination, "third world countries" must "decrease their population numbers" in accord with the principles of "environmentalism." The statement poses population decline in "the third world" as an ecological imperative: "fewer people equals less pollution. Ultimately, that is the only way to reduce global pollution."[49] This confused reasoning is the impetus behind the growing turn to eco-nationalism on the American far right, and an uncomfortable indication of the diminishing space between extreme and mainstream viewpoints. Alt-right arguments along these lines are dismayingly similar to the stances held by "overwhelmingly white, Western, and affluent environmentalists that frame population control in the Global South as a potential solution for climate change."[50]

The fixation on population is one of the core themes of right-wing ecology that carry considerable potential for mainstream crossover. With or without direct racial overtones, it is frequently paired with wistful visions of simplicity and rootedness founded on the hardy image of "agrarianism as an alternative to industrial civilization."[51] This populist agrarian tendency represents a "potent form of ruralism with roots in romantic and conservative notions of an organic society," including "a critique of industrialisation, urbanisation and modernity based on nostalgia for a vanishing way of life."[52] Far right intrusions into seemingly progressive spaces may seem less baffling in light of that background. In a 2019 US incident that made national headlines, local self-sufficiency collided with white supremacy at a farmers market in an Indiana college town; protests erupted when the proprietors of an organic family farm were revealed as members of the alt-right group Identity Evropa.[53] Behind the headlines lies an increasingly commonplace trend. For many so-called identitarians, natural foods and healthy soil are essential steps toward the regeneration of racial consciousness.

Nature takes a prominent place in the ideological profile of the alt-right, where ecological awareness is meant to "encourage an organic and fruitful relationship to the homeland."[54] On anonymous internet forums, alt-right followers make proud appeals to "blood and soil" and "Lebensraum" while promoting wilderness preserves and bioregionalism. They denounce "overpopulation" and "multiculturalism" and identify strongly with deep ecology, animal rights, and veganism.[55] Many of these younger partisans of the refurbished far right refer to themselves as "white nationalists" when proselytizing for a green agenda. Although it has become the standard designation among scholars as well as journalists, "white nationalist" is a problematic term in several ways. White power proponents themselves prefer the label as a way to gain easier access to mainstream discourse and distance their views from the unwelcome connotations of "white supremacist." Moreover, "white nationalist" does not fully capture the white power scene in the contemporary United States, much of which has little concern for an American nation, however conceived, but sees the US state itself as an obstacle to the white power cause; these strands of the movement are better understood as racialist rather than nationalist. Current alt-rightists and identitarians hailing "blood and soil" rely on this ambiguity in framing their message.

Preceding generations of the US radical right likewise affirmed "communion with Nature" as vital to white racial awakening. In the 1970s the program of the National Socialist White People's Party demanded "the phasing out of all forms of energy which befoul the environment, such as petroleum and nuclear fuels."[56] The 1980s manifesto "Aryan Destiny: Back to the Land" by Jost Turner, founder of the National Socialist Kindred, called for "living simply like our ancestors" through "organic gardens" and "herbal medicines"; this would allow white people "to begin a new life, a simple, joyful, Aryan life, close to nature, and away from the degeneracy of the urban cesspools."[57] Tom Metzger's group White Aryan Resistance repeatedly highlighted environmental topics and applauded Earth First!, avowing that "Ecology is for Aryans."[58] By the 1990s neo-Nazi terrorist David Lane warned that increasing population was "ruining the topsoil, depleting the forests, exhausting the fossil fuels and producing nuclear wastelands." If left unchecked, "the industrialization of the third world by capitalists" would "quickly destroy the planet." Lane held that "materialism" is "unnatural" and "ultimately leads to conspicuous, unnecessary consumption, which in turn leads to the rape of Nature and destruction of the environment."[59]

From defending the "natural order" to defeating the "immigrant invasion," from acclaiming environmentalism as an "Aryan" movement to "living on the land in harmony with nature," from "conserving the environment" to "conserving the White race," the ideology of blood and soil arises again and again throughout the spectrum of right-wing ecological politics. While many of its devotees long for a full-fledged ecofascism, the decisive assumptions can just as easily appear in non-fascist form.[60] Under the impact of the anti-immigrant massacres in Christchurch and El Paso, however, public attention has understandably centered on the extreme right and its preoccupation with the natural world.

The perpetrator of the March 2019 Christchurch attack described himself as an "eco-fascist" in the disjointed manifesto he posted online, allotting large sections of the document to environmental affairs. Despite legitimate concerns about giving the perpetrator undue publicity, the text merits critical scrutiny.[61] Under the heading "Green nationalism is the only true nationalism," the manifesto lamented "the continued destruction of the natural environment" through "mass immigration and uncontrolled urbanization." Juxtaposing noble European nature and the imagined threat to its integrity, the petulant essay proclaimed: "Continued immigration into Europe is environmental warfare and ultimately destructive to nature itself. The Europe of the future is not one of concrete and steel, smog and wires but a place of forests, lakes, mountains and meadows." Unless the "enemies of our race" are stopped, the "natural environment" will continue to be "industrialized, pulverized and commoditized." This will lead inexorably to "ever expanding cities and shrinking forests, a complete removal of man from nature" as well as the "racial and cultural replacement of the European people." As if to justify his slaughter of fifty-one peaceful children and adults, the perpetrator urged: "The invaders are the ones over populating the world. Kill the invaders, kill the overpopulation and by doing so save the environment."[62]

Though the mass shootings in Christchurch and El Paso shocked the world, the myths that motivated them are readily recognizable. They reprise a set of timeworn convictions that have circulated on both the mainstream right and the extreme right for many years. Aside from showing that online prattle can have tragic consequences in the real world, these events revealed overlapping ideas and ongoing interactions between the far right fringe and the political center. Due to the remarkably malleable nature of "environmentalism's broad appeal," the typical incoherence of right-wing ecology need not be an obstacle to its spread.[63] From YouTube channels to high literature, fascist traces can emerge in unlikely corners of environmental thought and practice, admonishing us to heed neglected lessons about the heritage of blood and soil.[64] In a world of mobile ideologies, "the dangerous discourses that often come from far right political tendencies can also easily permeate conservative and center-right groups as well as mainstream political life."[65]

Confronting this challenge calls for more than historical reconstruction of abstruse theories about population and purity. Like any effort to counter the far right, it will require a combination of research and resistance, of education and active engagement, in order to disrupt the manifold links between historical naiveté and political complacency. The widely accepted view of environmentalism as a "white movement," for instance, ignores the integral part that activists of color have played in environmental struggles around the globe, from the Chipko movement in India to the Green Belt movement in Kenya, from Ken Saro-Wiwa in Nigeria to Berta Cáceres in Honduras. It ignores the centuries-long history of African American and Native American ecological conservation and environmental activism, and it ignores the diversity of green endeavors today.[66] Espousing a whitewashed past, apologists for the right leave these prejudices unquestioned.

Their critics sometimes give in to the opposite temptation. Two errors commonly arise in this context, among liberal commentators and others. One is to assume that right-wing anti-immigrant environmental sentiments are somehow not really environmentalist. Unfortunately that malignant tradition is just as much a part of the history of ecological politics as its left-wing alternatives. It is not merely a cover for something else. The other error is to deem radical rightists opponents of everything the Western tradition stands for. What far right groups actually represent is an exaggerated version of tendencies that have been at the heart of European and American societies for centuries, tendencies that form a central part of our shared past and fractured present.

In its ecological dimensions, the current drift toward the extreme right stems not only from the deep reservoirs of irrationality in human social life but from the longing to make whole what has been broken. Thus the backward-looking and forward-looking strands in far right thinking are not as incompatible as they may seem; they are not diametrically opposed but dialectically intertwined. Far right believers frequently adopt both a reactionary stance and a radical stance at the same time.[67] They yearn for a lost past—an entirely imaginary but no less powerful image of a lost past, of a long gone golden age, an earlier era of glory and grandeur, a return to harmony and simplicity, to healthy and intact community— just as they yearn for a radically different future: a future that will be unlike anything previously seen, that will resolve all the troubles of modern life, that will bring forth something wholly original, a new order of being, a new form of living, a radiant future of promise, peace, and lasting prosperity, a future that cannot even be conceived from the debased present. For the far right, these two poles form a distorted dialectic, a radical-reactionary vision of revival, renewal, reawakening, of reaching toward ultimate fulfillment and an exhilarating destiny that will surpass all that has come before.

For those committed to thwarting the deadly dreams of far right triumph, it is crucial to understand the wellsprings that feed such hopes and fears even as we interrogate the myths on which they subsist. Among the most tenacious of those myths is the spurious connection between immigration and environmental degradation. This idea is not just socially abhorrent, it is ecologically absurd. Growing levels of migration are a result, not a cause, of the global climate crisis, and the arbitrary nature of international boundaries makes a mockery of any attempt to ward off ecological damage by targeting immigrant communities. Climate change does not halt at national borders. Yet pointing out the discrepancies in right-wing logic is not enough. We will need to offer more than a counterargument; we will need to create an inclusive public culture rooted in a radical social and ecological vision, emancipatory and egalitarian, that can inspire resilience in place of resentment.

There is much more work to be done in coming to terms with "the convergence of right-wing extremism and environmentalism."[68] In making sense of a bewildering world, our best tools are critical inquiry and conscientious reflection. It will not help to pretend that blood and soil loyalties are a thing of the past, or that far right fantasies are trivial and unworthy of sustained examination. The rise of formerly peripheral figures like Mussolini and Hitler shows that under the right historical conditions, fascist initiatives can quickly move from the margins to the mainstream. In or out of power, their record indicates how near the supposed extremes of Fascism and Nazism were to the center of society.[69] As the unsteady orbit of the far right shifts in the face of worldwide environmental calamity, it will become more urgent than ever to respond creatively and courageously. Constructing an ecological future means standing against exclusion and embracing solidarity in a world that has a place for all.

Notes

1   See the thoughtful analysis by Natasha Lennard, "The El Paso Shooter Embraced Eco-Fascism. We Can't Let the Far Right Co-Opt the Environmental Struggle" *The Intercept* August 5, 2019; cf. Alexander Kaufman, "The El Paso Manifesto: Where Racism and Eco-Fascism Meet" *Mother Jones* August 5, 2019, and Jeff Sparrow, "Eco-fascists and the ugly fight for 'our way of life' as the environment disintegrates" *Guardian* November 29, 2019. Online sources cited in this essay were accessed in June 2020. Several of them come from manifestos posted by perpetrators of mass shootings; I have refrained from providing links to the original text.

2   The phrase "Blut und Boden" appeared in *völkisch* contexts as early as 1924, though the conjoined terms can be found in texts from a decade or more before that; for examples see Horst Gies, *Richard Walther Darré: Der "Reichsbauernführer", die nationalsozialistische "Blut und Boden"-Ideologie und die Machteroberung Hitlers* (Cologne: Böhlau, 2019), 216, 251, 342, 493. After the Nazis came to power in 1933 the phrase began to appear in English in reports from Germany in the *Times* of London and the *New York Times*.

3   Thomas Robertson, *The Malthusian Moment: Global Population Growth and the Birth of American Environmentalism* (New Brunswick: Rutgers University Press, 2012), 198. Other studies note that Tanton stood "at the heart of the white nationalist movement" (Robert Sussman, *The Myth of Race: The Troubling Persistence of an Unscientific Idea*, Harvard University Press 2014, 287), while the groups he founded have been characterized as "virulently racist" (Noel Sturgeon, *Environmentalism in Popular Culture: Gender, Race, Sexuality, and the Politics of the Natural*, University of Arizona

Press 2009, 143). See also Noah Lanard, "Architect of Modern Nativism Dies, but His Ideas Have New Life Under Trump" *Mother Jones* July 19, 2019; Susie Cagle, "The environmentalist roots of anti-immigrant bigotry" Guardian August 16, 2019; Sonia Shah, *The Next Great Migration: The Beauty and Terror of Life on the Move* (New York: Bloomsbury, 2020), 154-88.

4 Sebastian Normandin and Sean Valles, "How a network of conservationists and population control activists created the contemporary US anti-immigration movement" *Endeavour* 39 (2015), 95-105. The Federation for American Immigration Reform, which Tanton founded, is "the largest and most influential immigration control organization in the United States and one of the most active groups maintaining the links between immigration and environmental politics [...] The organization's leadership is a Who's Who of American eugenicists and respectable racists." (Lisa Sun-Hee Park and David Naguib Pellow, *The Slums of Aspen: Immigrants vs. the Environment in America's Eden*, New York University Press 2011, 131). Cf. William Tucker, *The Funding of Scientific Racism* (Urbana: University of Illinois Press, 2002), 188-94; Leonard Zeskind, "The New Nativism: The Alarming Overlap between White Nationalists and Mainstream Anti-Immigrant Forces" *American Prospect* November 2005, 15-18; Elena Gutiérrez, *Fertile Matters: The Politics of Mexican-Origin Women's Reproduction* (Austin: University of Texas Press, 2008), 73-93; Jenny Levison et al., "Apply the Brakes: Anti-immigrant Co-optation of the Environmental Movement" (Center for New Community, 2010); Heidi Beirich, "Greenwash: Nativists, Environmentalism & the Hypocrisy of Hate" (Southern Poverty Law Center, 2010); Brentin Mock, "The Green Movement Is Talking About Racism? It's About Time" *Outside Online* February

27, 2017; Brian Calvert, "The road to ecofascism is paved with green intentions" *High Country News* April 1, 2020.

5   John Hultgren, *Border Walls Gone Green: Nature and Anti-Immigrant Politics in America* (Minneapolis: University of Minnesota Press, 2015), 86. Betsy Hartmann identifies Hardin as a leading influence on the "fascistic wing" of "population environmentalism" (Hartmann, *Reproductive Rights and Wrongs: The Global Politics of Population Control*, South End Press 1995, 142). For context see Eric Ross, *The Malthus Factor: Poverty, Politics and Population in Capitalist Development* (London: Zed, 1998), 73-78, 201-13; Rajani Bhatia, "Greening the Swastika: Nativism and Anti-Semitism in the Population and Environment Debate" in Jael Silliman and Anannya Bhattacharjee, eds., *Policing the National Body: Race, Gender, and Criminalization* (Boston: South End Press, 2002), 291-321; Ian Angus and Simon Butler, *Too Many People? Population, Immigration, and the Environmental Crisis* (Chicago: Haymarket, 2011), 109-21; Alex Amend, "First as Tragedy, Then as Fascism: Ecologist Garrett Hardin's enduring gift to the nativist right" *The Baffler* September 26, 2019. Deep ecologists continue to promote anti-immigrant ideologues like Hardin and Tanton; see e.g. Philip Cafaro and Eileen Crist, eds., *Life on the Brink: Environmentalists Confront Overpopulation* (Athens: University of Georgia Press, 2012).

6   For a detailed account see Miles Powell, *Vanishing America: Species Extinction, Racial Peril, and the Origins of Conservation* (Cambridge: Harvard University Press, 2016); cf. Susan Schrepfer, *The Fight to Save the Redwoods: A History of Environmental Reform, 1917-1978* (Madison: University of Wisconsin Press, 1983), 42-46; Alexandra Minna Stern, *Eugenic Nation: Faults and Frontiers of Better Breeding in Modern America* (Berkeley:

University of California Press, 2005), 115-49; Adam Rome, "Nature Wars, Culture Wars: Immigration and Environmental Reform in the Progressive Era" *Environmental History* 13 (2008), 432-53; Charles Wohlforth, "Conservation and Eugenics: The environmental movement's dirty secret" *Orion Magazine* July 2010. This phenomenon is not uniquely American; similar dynamics have arisen around the world, from environmentalist hostility toward immigrants to the expulsion of indigenous communities in the name of nature conservation. Compare Roderick Neumann, *Imposing Wilderness: Struggles over Livelihood and Nature Preservation in Africa* (Berkeley: University of California Press, 2002); Ramachandra Guha, "The Authoritarian Biologist and the Arrogance of Anti-humanism: Wildlife Conservation in the Third World" in Vasant Saberwal, ed., *Battles Over Nature: Science and the Politics of Conservation* (Delhi: Permanent Black, 2003), 139-57; Mark Dowie, *Conservation Refugees: The Hundred-Year Conflict between Global Conservation and Native Peoples* (Cambridge: MIT Press, 2009); Arun Agrawal and Kent Redford, "Conservation and Displacement: An Overview" *Conservation and Society* 7 (2009), 1-10.

7   Dan Stone, "Rolf Gardiner: An Honorary Nazi?" in Stone, *The Holocaust, Fascism and Memory* (New York: Palgrave Macmillan, 2013), 96-109, Gardiner quoted on 107. Stone goes on to observe that Gardiner's "role in the early organic movement was driven as much by the idea of racial regeneration through contact with the national soil as by environmental concerns; indeed, the two elements of his thought are inseparable." (107) Cf. Thomas Linehan, *British Fascism, 1918-39: Parties, Ideology and Culture* (Manchester: Manchester University Press, 2000), 138-42, 245-68; Mike Tyldesley, "The German Youth Movement and National

Socialism: Some Views from Britain" *Journal of Contemporary History* 41 (2006), 21-34; Matthew Reed, *Rebels for the Soil: The Rise of the Global Organic Food and Farming Movement* (London: Earthscan, 2010), 45-47, 57-59.

8   Dan Stone, "The English Array, the BUF and the Dilemmas of British Fascism" *Journal of Modern History* 75 (2003), 336-58; Richard Moore-Colyer, "Towards 'Mother Earth': Jorian Jenks, Organicism, the Right and the British Union of Fascists" *Journal of Contemporary History* 39 (2004), 353-71; Philip Conford, "Organic Society: Agriculture and Radical Politics in the Career of Gerard Wallop, Ninth Earl of Portsmouth (1898-1984)" *Agricultural History Review* 53 (2005), 78-96; Gregory Barton, *The Global History of Organic Farming* (Oxford: Oxford University Press, 2018), 33-39.

9   Publisher's description for Jorian Jenks, *Spring Comes Again* (London: Sanctuary Press, 2019); the original edition appeared in 1939. See also the historical study by Philip Coupland, *Farming, Fascism and Ecology: A Life of Jorian Jenks* (London: Routledge, 2016). E. F. Schumacher, later President of the Soil Association, was involved in pro-Nazi activities in the US and the UK in his youth; see the account by his daughter Barbara Wood, *E.F. Schumacher: His Life and Thought* (New York: Harper & Row, 1984), 54-59.

10 2010 BNP program quoted in Kristian Voss, "Nature and Nation in Harmony: The Ecological Component of Far Right Ideology" (dissertation, European University Institute, 2014), 102 and 157; cf. Emily Turner-Graham, "'Protecting our green and pleasant land': UKIP, the BNP and a history of green ideology on Britain's far right" in Bernhard Forchtner, ed., *The Far Right and the Environment: Politics, Discourse and Communication* (London: Routledge, 2019), 57-71.

11 Quotations from Southgate are taken from the 2013 "Interview
    with Troy Southgate" posted at the far right NoWhereNews site.
    See also the chapter "Blood & Soil: Revolutionary Nationalism as
    the Vanguard of Ecological Sanity" in Troy Southgate, *Tradition &*
    Revolution (London: Arktos, 2010).

12 "Interview with Troy Southgate." Southgate continues: "I am a
    great critic of technology itself. I agree with John Zerzan that
    modern civilisation is a pestilence that has dragged mankind out
    of its environment […]" Southgate's "National Anarchist" website
    features prominent sections on "ecology" and "animal liberation,"
    including links to the Soil Association, Earth First!, John Michell,
    and the Unabomber Manifesto. Critical accounts include Graham
    Macklin, "Co-opting the counter culture: Troy Southgate and the
    National Revolutionary Faction" *Patterns of Prejudice* 39 (2005),
    301-26, and Spencer Sunshine, "Rebranding Fascism: National-
    Anarchists" *The Public Eye* Winter 2008.

13 See the informative report by *Searchlight* archivist Daniel Jones,
    "Greenshirts—The (Mis)use of Environmentalism by the Extreme
    Right" *History Workshop Online* April 21, 2020. On the long
    history of left alternatives see Peter Gould, *Early Green Politics:*
    Back to Nature, Back to the Land, and Socialism in Britain,
    1880-1900 (New York: St. Martin's Press, 1988), and Raymond
    Williams, "Socialism and Ecology" in Williams, *Resources of Hope*
    (London: Verso, 1989), 210-26.

14 Venus Bivar, *Organic Resistance: The Struggle over Industrial Farming*
    in Postwar France (Chapel Hill: University of North Carolina Press,
    2018), 4; cf. 50-52, 58-61, 67-72. Compare the partially contrasting
    case study by Chaia Heller, *Food, Farms & Solidarity: French*
    Farmers Challenge Industrial Agriculture and Genetically Modified
    Crops (Durham: Duke University Press, 2013). On Germany

see Corinna Treitel, "Triumph of the Till: The Organic Food Movement's Nazi Past" *World Policy Journal* 35 (2018), 83-87.

15 Kate Aronoff, "The European Far Right's Environmental Turn" *Dissent* May 31, 2019; Norimitsu Onishi, "France's Far Right Wants to Be an Environmental Party, Too" *New York Times* October 18, 2019, A5.

16 1993 National Front program quoted in Voss, "Nature and Nation in Harmony," 102. For extended discussion of the party's environmental stands see Peter Davies, *The National Front in France: Ideology, Discourse, and Power* (London: Routledge, 1999), 107-12, 202-07. Brief background on earlier French traditions of "blood and soil" can be found in Zeev Sternhell, *Neither Right nor Left: Fascist Ideology in France* (Princeton: Princeton University Press, 1996), xxxiii-xxxiv, 25-26.

17 Caterina Froio et al., *CasaPound Italia: Contemporary Extreme-Right Politics* (London: Routledge, 2020), 50-52; Giorgia Bulli, "Environmental politics on the Italian far right" in Forchtner, ed., *The Far Right and the Environment*, 88-103. Bulli notes that "environmentalist associations play a major role" in Casa Pound's "self-representation as a lively social movement." (97)

18 Bulli, "Environmental politics on the Italian far right," 97. On Casa Pound's neo-fascist form of forest conservation see Erica Eisen, "Italy's Green Fascists" *Jewish Currents* September 18, 2019.

19 Statement from the Freiheitliche Partei Österreichs quoted in Kristian Voss, "The ecological component of the ideology and legislative activity of the Freedom Party of Austria" in Forchtner, ed., *The Far Right and the Environment*, 177. Voss highlights anti-anthropocentrism and organicism as the core of the FPÖ's stance on animal welfare and nature protection, tied directly to the party's "ethnic nationalist framework" (ibid.)

20 Voss, "Nature and Nation in Harmony," 18.

21 Damir Skenderovic, *The Radical Right in Switzerland* (New York: Berghahn, 2009), 206-14, quote on 210.

22 2016 Nordic Resistance Movement manifesto quoted in Maria Darwish, "Green neo-Nazism: Examining the intersection of masculinity, far-right extremism and environmentalism in the Nordic Resistance Movement" (MA thesis, University of Oslo, 2018), 1.

23 See the overview of the "Green Wing for Racial Humanism and Ecological Consciousness" at the Golden Dawn International Newsroom site; its motto is "We fight for the Race, and the Nature that nourished it."

24 Veronica Davidov, "Beyond formal environmentalism: Eco-nationalism and the 'Ringing Cedars' of Russia" *Culture, Agriculture, Food and Environment* 37 (2015), 2-13; Rasa Pranskeviciute, "The 'Back to Nature' Worldview in Nature-based Spirituality Movements: The Case of the Anastasians" in James Lewis, ed., *Handbook of Nordic New Religions* (Leiden: Brill, 2015), 441-56; Julia Andreeva, "Verbal Clichés of Followers in the 'Anastasia' New Religious Movement" *Anthropology & Archeology of Eurasia* 57 (2018), 88-106.

25 See the website of the movement's branch in Saxony, lebensraumsachsen.de: "Wir schaffen Lebensraum der Zukunft." Press reports include Andreas Weller, "Rechte Biobauern und ihre Vorbilder: Die Neonazi-Szene breitet sich unter Gärtnern aus" *Sächsische Zeitung* June 19, 2018; Lisa Forster, "'Anastasia'-Bewegung: Rechte Tendenzen in der Esoterik" *Mitteldeutsche Zeitung* March 12, 2019; Andreas Speit, "Völkische Expansion: Neonazis suchen Lebensraum" *die tageszeitung* November 22, 2019. In English compare Susan Richards, "The fairy tale that gripped Russia" *Financial Times* August 14, 2009, and Peter Paul

Catterall, "Green nationalism? How the far right could learn to love the environment" *The Ecologist* April 12, 2017. As Catterall observes, "Myths of a pagan past in harmony with nature have been a feature of green nationalism, from its beginnings through to the Anastasia ecovillages in contemporary Russia where, unlike their equivalent hippy communes found in the West, sustainable living is combined with a 'reactionary eco-nationalism.'"

26 Vladimir Megré, *The Book of Kin* (Kahului: Ringing Cedars Press, 2008), 148-66. Critical assessments of the movement are available in German; see e.g. Tim Schulz, "Rechte Esoteriker: Anastasia in Ostsachsen" *Endstation Rechts* June 16, 2019; Marius Hellwig, "Söhne und Töchter der Taiga: Zur völkisch-esoterischen Anastasia-Bewegung" in Sina Franz, ed., *Love Nature. Not Fascism* (Berlin: Fachstelle Radikalisierungsprävention und Engagement im Naturschutz, 2019), 10-12; Carl Kinsky and Sebastian Hell, "Ökologie, Rassenlehre und Antisemitismus: Die 'Anastasia-Bewegung' in Hessen" *Lotta* February 2020, 25-27.

27 Stéphane François, "The Euro-Pagan Scene: Between Paganism and Radical Right" *Journal for the Study of Radicalism* 1 (2007), 35-54; Ulrike Heß-Meining, "Right-Wing Esotericism in Europe" in Uwe Backes ed., *The Extreme Right in Europe* (Göttingen: Vandenhoeck & Ruprecht, 2012), 383-408; Jean-Yves Camus and Nicolas Lebourg, *Far-Right Politics in Europe* (Cambridge: Harvard University Press, 2017), 141-44, 166-70.

28 Amy Hale, "John Michell, Radical Traditionalism, and the Emerging Politics of the Pagan New Right" *The Pomegranate: International Journal of Pagan Studies* 13 (2011), 77-97.

29 Stefanie von Schnurbein, *Norse Revival: Transformations of Germanic Neopaganism* (Leiden: Brill, 2016), 215; see her discerning discussion of "Asatru—A Religion of Nature?" on 180-

215. Austrian author Reinhard Farkas, an exponent of *völkisch* ecology, presents a typical example of the political confusion that marks this milieu. His book on the spiritual roots of green thought mixes together esotericism, neo-paganism, holism, and life reform, celebrating antisemites like Theodor Fritsch and Guido List along with theosophy, anthroposophy, and ariosophy: Reinhard Farkas, *Grüne Wurzeln: Ökologische und spirituelle Reform in der Steiermark* (Fohnsdorf: Podmenik, 1992), 56-66, 102-03, 145-46. For critical analysis see Heribert Schiedel, "'Mutter Erde' statt 'Blut und Boden': Die ökologisch-spirituelle Erneuerung des Faschismus" in Wolfgang Purtscheller, ed., *Die Ordnung, die sie meinen: "Neue Rechte" in Österreich* (Vienna: Picus, 1994), 124-49.

30   White Order of Thule member and Pagan Liberation League founder Nathan Pett quoted in Mattias Gardell, *Gods of the Blood: The Pagan Revival and White Separatism* (Durham: Duke University Press, 2003), 312. Pett later renounced white supremacy; see the interview with him titled "Tainted Thule" in the *Southern Poverty Law Center Intelligence Report* Spring 2011, 30-31.

31   Gardell, *Gods of the Blood*, 313. Gardell reports that radical right pagan revivalists viewed Dave Foreman, Paul Watson, and David Brower as "influential ecologists moving toward a racist position." On the international context cf. Stefanie von Schnurbein, "Religion of Nature or Racist Cult? Contemporary Neogermanic Pagan Movements in Germany" in Uwe Puschner, ed., *Antisemitismus, Paganismus, Völkische Religion* (Munich: Saur, 2004), 135-49; Egil Asprem, "Heathens Up North: Politics, Polemics, and Contemporary Norse Paganism in Norway" *The Pomegranate* 10 (2008), 41-69; Graham Harvey, "Contemporary Paganism and the Occult" in Christopher Partridge, ed., *The Occult World* (New York: Routledge, 2015), 361-71; Michael

Strmiska, "Pagan Politics in the 21st Century: 'Peace and Love' or 'Blood and Soil'?" *The Pomegranate* 20 (2018), 5-44.

32 For informative overviews see Amy Hale, "Marketing 'Rad Trad': The Growing Co-Influence Between Paganism and the New Right" in Taylor Ellwood, ed., *Bringing Race to the Table: Exploring Racism in the Pagan Community* (London: Immanion Press, 2015), 103-21; Shannon Weber, "White Supremacy's Old Gods: The Far Right and Neopaganism" *The Public Eye* Winter 2018; Kaarina Aitamurto, "The Rise of Paganism and the Far Right in Europe" *Oxford Research Encyclopedias: Religion,* May 2020.

33 Henning Köhler, *Arbeitsdienst in Deutschland: Pläne und Verwirklichungsformen bis zur Einführung der Arbeitsdienstpflicht im Jahre 1935* (Berlin: Duncker & Humblot, 1967), 39-42; Gerhard Rempel, *Hitler's Children: The Hitler Youth and the SS* (Chapel Hill: University of North Carolina Press, 1989), 107-10; Klaus Mües-Baron, *Heinrich Himmler—Aufstieg des Reichsführers SS (1900-1933)* (Göttingen: Vandenhoeck & Ruprecht, 2011), 355-71; Stefan Brauckmann, "Historische Hintergründe: Die Artamanenbewegung in der Weimarer Republik" in Toralf Staud, ed., *Braune Ökologen* (Berlin: Heinrich Böll Stiftung, 2012), 39-50; Christian Niemeyer, *Die dunklen Seiten der Jugendbewegung: Vom Wandervogel zur Hitlerjugend* (Tübingen: Francke, 2013), 52-63; Rüdiger Ahrens, *Bündische Jugend: Eine neue Geschichte, 1918-1933* (Göttingen: Wallstein, 2015).

34 George Mosse, *The Crisis of German Ideology: Intellectual Origins of the Third Reich* (New York: Grosset & Dunlap, 1964), 108-25; Ulrich Linse, "Antiurbane Bestrebungen in der Weimarer Republik" in Peter Alter, ed., *Im Banne der Metropolen* (Göttingen: Vandenhoeck &. Ruprecht, 1993), 314-47; Uwe Puschner, "'One People, One Reich, One God': The Völkische

Weltanschauung and Movement" *Bulletin of the German
Historical Institute London* 24 (2002), 5-27; Bodo Kahmann,
"Antisemitism and Antiurbanism, Past and Present: Empirical
and Theoretical Approaches" in Alvin Rosenfeld, ed., *Deciphering
the New Antisemitism* (Bloomington: Indiana University
Press, 2015), 482-507. Statements from Artamanen members
include Bruno Tanzmann, "Aufbruch der Artamanen" *Deutsche
Bauernhochschule* Summer 1924, 1-6; Fritz Hugo Hoffmann,
"Artam" *Nordische Blätter: Zeitschrift für nordisches Leben* April
1928, 33-35; Rudolf Proksch, "Artamanen: Der Beginn einer
Bewegung zur Heimkehr der Jugend aufs Land" *Wille und Macht*
March 1939, 16-28.

35 Marcus Schmidt, "Steine sammeln für ein neues Leben" *Junge
Freiheit* April 8, 2005, a celebratory portrait of a "neo-Artamanen"
settlement in Mecklenburg published in a major far right journal.
For critical press coverage cf. Andreas Speit, "Die grünen
Braunen" *die tageszeitung* October 23, 2007; Jens Griesbach,
"Artamanen auf dem Vormarsch?" *Schweriner Volkszeitung*
November 15, 2007; Sebastian Beck, "Rechtsextremismus in
Deutschland: Wo der Nachbar Nazi ist" *Süddeutsche Zeitung*
February 7, 2011; Edwin Baumgartner, "Bio, Blut und Boden"
Wiener Zeitung July 6, 2016; Dietmar Neuerer, "Tiefbrauner
Osten" *Handelsblatt* September 20, 2016; Tonia Mastrobuoni,
"Viaggio in Germania nel paradiso degli econazisti" *La
Repubblica* October 13, 2016; Edith Kresta, "Die rechte Landlust"
die tageszeitung January 15, 2017.

36 Stefan Brauckmann, "Nach dem Vorbild der Artamanen:
Völkische Siedlungsbewegung" in Anke Oxenfarth, ed., *Ökologie
von rechts: Braune Umweltschützer auf Stimmenfang* (Munich:
Oekom, 2012), 52-58; Ulrich Linse, "Völkisch-jugendbewegte

Siedlungen im 20. und 21. Jahrhundert" in Gideon Botsch, ed., *Jugendbewegung, Antisemitismus und rechtsradikale Politik: Vom 'Freideutschen Jugendtag' bis zur Gegenwart* (Berlin: de Gruyter, 2014), 29-73; Andreas Förster, "Öko und Rechts: Wie 'völkische Siedler' ganze Dörfer unterwandern" *Berliner Zeitung* December 28, 2014; Zoé Sona, "Jung, naturverbunden, rechts: Ökonazis im Wendland" *die tageszeitung* May 13, 2015.

37 Compare Voss, "Nature and Nation in Harmony," 108-117; Thomas Jahn and Peter Wehling, *Ökologie von rechts: Nationalismus und Umweltschutz bei der Neuen Rechten und den "Republikanern"* (Frankfurt: Campus, 1990), 92-97; Christoph Busch, "Das Grün im Braun: Umweltschutz in den Parteiprogrammen der deutschen extremen Rechten" *Jahrbuch für Extremismus- und Terrorismusforschung* 5 (2012), 246-80; Johannes Melchert, "Ökologie und Naturschutz in der NPD" in Gudrun Heinrich, ed., *Naturschutz und Rechtsradikalismus: Gegenwärtige Entwicklungen, Probleme, Abgrenzungen* (Bonn: Bundesamt für Naturschutz, 2015), 123-27.

38 *Umwelt & Aktiv: Das Magazin für ganzheitliches Denken, Umweltschutz, Tierschutz, Heimatschutz*, in print from 2007 to 2019, now online. Though formally independent—it is published by the "Midgard Society"—the magazine had close ties to the NPD since it first appeared. A tacit successor, *Die Kehre: Zeitschrift für Naturschutz*, debuted in early 2020. Cf. Andreas Speit, "U&A: Das Ökologiemagazin der Rechten" in Oxenfarth, ed., *Ökologie von rechts*, 65-71; Madeleine Hurd and Steffen Werther, "The Militant Media of Neo-Nazi Environmentalism" in Heike Graf, ed., *The Environment in the Age of the Internet* (Cambridge: Open Book, 2016), 137-70; Nils Franke, *Die Natur des rechtsextremistischen Lebensstils: Eine kritische Analyse*

(Mainz: Landeszentrale für Umweltaufklärung, 2017); Bernhard
Forchtner, "Nation, nature, purity: Extreme-right biodiversity in
Germany" *Patterns of Prejudice* 53 (2019), 285-301.

39 Noteworthy examples include Philipp Wittrock, "Siegeszug
    der braunen Siedler" *Der Spiegel* September 26, 2006; Alan
    Posener, "Die netten Ökofaschisten" *Welt am Sonntag* December
    12, 2010; Karen Grass, "Rechtsextreme Umweltschützer"
    die tageszeitung January 13, 2012; Christian Pfaffinger,
    "Braune Bio-Kameradschaft" *Der Spiegel* April 3, 2012;
    Anna Schmidt, *Völkische Siedler/innen im ländlichen Raum*
    (Berlin: Amadeu-Antonio-Stiftung, 2014); Nils Franke,
    Naturschutz gegen Rechtsextremismus (Mainz: Landeszentrale
    für Umweltaufklärung, 2016); Lisa Schnell, "Bayerns ach so
    harmlose Öko-Nazis" *Süddeutsche Zeitung* August 17, 2017;
    Lukas Nicolaisen, ed., *Rechtsextreme Ideologien im Natur- und
    Umweltschutz* (Berlin: Naturfreunde Deutschlands, 2018);
    Andrea Röpke and Andreas Speit, *Völkische Landnahme: Alte
    Sippen, junge Siedler, rechte Ökos* (Berlin: Links, 2019); Hans-
    Gerd Marian und Michael Müller, "Der Kampf um Lebensraum:
    Braune Ideologen im Umwelt- und Naturschutz" *Blätter für
    deutsche und internationale Politik* February 2020, 81-89.

40 Andreas Speit, "Völkische Erweckung: Die Natur- und
    Tierliebe von Paul Förster" in Heinrich, ed., *Naturschutz und
    Rechtsradikalismus*, 62-72; Miriam Zerbel, "Tierschutzbewegung"
    in Uwe Puschner, ed., *Handbuch zur 'Völkischen Bewegung' 1871-
    1918* (Munich: Saur, 1996), 546-57; Uwe Puschner, *Die völkische
    Bewegung im wilhelminischen Kaiserreich: Sprache, Rasse, Religion*
    (Darmstadt: Wissenschaftliche Buchgesellschaft, 2001), 166-
    70. Förster was not an exception; comparable figures within
    the nineteenth and twentieth century German environmental

milieu include Gustav Simons, Hermann Löns, Paul Schultze-Naumburg, Karl Strünckmann, and Werner Altpeter. Their twenty-first century successors are well aware of this lineage and proudly point to it as evidence that ecological politics properly belong to the right; for a classic instance see the nostalgic survey by the late far right author Norbert Borrmann, "Ökologie ist rechts" *Sezession* October 2013, 4-7.

41 Nils Franke, "Personelle und institutionelle Kontinuitäten im Naturschutz aus der Zeit des Nationalsozialismus in die frühe Bundesrepublik" in Heinrich, ed., *Naturschutz und Rechtsradikalismus*, 100-07; Kai Hünemörder, *Die Frühgeschichte der globalen Umweltkrise und die Formierung der deutschen Umweltpolitik (1950-1973)* (Stuttgart: Steiner, 2004), 28-30; Willi Oberkrome, *Deutsche Heimat: Nationale Konzeption und regionale Praxis von Naturschutz, Landschaftsgestaltung und Kulturpolitik in Westfalen-Lippe und Thüringen 1900-1960* (Paderborn: Schöningh, 2004), 396-415; Jens Ivo Engels, *Naturpolitik in der Bundesrepublik: Ideenwelt und politische Verhaltensstile in Naturschutz und Umweltbewegung 1950-1980* (Paderborn: Schöningh, 2006), 46-55; Sandra Chaney, *Nature of the Miracle Years: Conservation in West Germany, 1945-1975* (New York: Berghahn, 2008), 48-53, 76-78; Axel Zutz, "Wege grüner Moderne: Praxis und Erfahrung der Landschaftsanwälte des NS-Staates zwischen 1930 und 1960" in Heinrich Mäding, ed., *Vom Dritten Reich zur Bundesrepublik* (Hannover: Akademie für Raumforschung und Landesplanung, 2009), 107-48; Hildegard Eissing, "Wer verfasste die 'Grüne Charta von der Mainau'? Einflüsse nationalsozialistischen Gedankengutes" *Naturschutz und Landschaftsplanung* 46 (2014), 247-52; Nils Franke and Uwe Pfenning, eds., *Kontinuitäten im Naturschutz* (Baden-Baden:

Nomos, 2014); Hans-Werner Frohn, ed., *Zum Umgang mit der NS-Vergangenheit im Naturschutz* (Munich: Oekom, 2019).

42 For a particularly unfortunate example see Frank Uekötter, *Deutschland in Grün: Eine zwiespältige Erfolgsgeschichte* (Göttingen: Vandenhoeck & Ruprecht, 2015), 72 and 244. Uekötter's work is otherwise more nuanced, but he is not alone among historians on this question. When confronted with critical scholarship on the subject, some of my colleagues prefer to comfort themselves with the notion that "left-wing nature lovers played a much larger role" than their right-wing counterparts in twentieth century Germany (John Williams, personal communication, October 5, 2014). It would be nice if this were true. In reality, however, until the 1970s such left versions of naturism were historically "rather marginal" (Engels, *Naturpolitik in der Bundesrepublik*, 39). Justus Ulbricht confirms that liberal and left engagement with ecological matters happened "only rarely" before the Nazi era, and that the predominance of right-wing nature protection continued after 1945: Ulbricht, "Die Heimat als Umwelt des Volkes: Ökologische Denkfiguren in Ideologie und Programmatik 'neurechter' Organisationen" in Richard Faber, ed., *Rechtsextremismus: Ideologie und Gewalt* (Berlin: Hentrich, 1995), 221-40, quote on 224. The same point is substantiated throughout much of the historical literature; see the balanced overview by Thomas Lekan, "From 'Naturschutz' to 'Umweltschutz': Nature Conservation and Environmental Reform in the Federal Republic of Germany, 1950-1980" *German Historical Institute Bulletin* 29 (2007), 68-95. For a case study of these dynamics during the Nazi era see Peter Staudenmaier, "Advocates for the Landscape: Alwin Seifert and Nazi Environmentalism" *German Studies Review* 43 (2020), 271-90.

43 Compare David Galbreath and Daunis Auers, "Green, Black

and Brown: Uncovering Latvia's Environmental Politics" *Journal of Baltic Studies* 40 (2009), 333-48; Mukul Sharma, *Green and Saffron: Hindu Nationalism and Indian Environmental Politics* (Ranikhet: Permanent Black, 2012); Richard Reitan, "Ecology and Japanese History: Reactionary Environmentalism's Troubled Relationship with the Past" *Asia-Pacific Journal* 15 (2017), 1-17; Ellen van Holstein and Lesley Head, "Shifting settler-colonial discourses of environmentalism: Representations of indigeneity and migration in Australian conservation" *Geoforum* 94 (2018), 41-52. On the ephemeral "Greenline Front," which claimed branches from Argentina to Belarus, see Bernhard Forchtner and Balša Lubarda, "Eco-fascism 'proper': The curious case of Greenline Front," Centre for Analysis of the Radical Right, June 25, 2020. African examples reveal a further aspect of blood and soil in practice; on colonial Rhodesia and apartheid South Africa see Barton, *The Global History of Organic Farming*, 130-32; JoAnn McGregor, "Conservation, Control and Ecological Change: The Politics and Ecology of Colonial Conservation in Zimbabwe" *Environment and History* 1 (1995), 257-79; Peter Delius and Stefan Schirmer, "Soil Conservation in a Racially Ordered Society: South Africa 1930-1970" *Journal of Southern African Studies* 26 (2000), 719-42; David Hughes, *Whiteness in Zimbabwe: Race, Landscape, and the Problem of Belonging* (New York: Palgrave Macmillan, 2010), 79-85; Simeon Maravanyika, "Soil Conservation and the White Agrarian Environment in Colonial Zimbabwe, c. 1908-1980" (dissertation, University of Pretoria, 2013); Yuka Suzuki, *The Nature of Whiteness: Race, Animals, and Nation in Zimbabwe* (University of Washington Press, 2017).

44 The exemplary research by Bernhard Forchtner and Hilary Moore offers thorough background on the complicated climate politics

of the European far right. See Bernhard Forchtner, "Extrem rechte Parteien im Klimawandel: Ein (kurzer) Blick auf die Schweiz, Österreich und Deutschland" in Heinrich, ed., *Naturschutz und Rechtsradikalismus*, 128-35; Bernhard Forchtner and Christoffer Kølvraa, "The Nature of Nationalism: Populist Radical Right Parties on Countryside and Climate" *Nature & Culture* 10 (2015), 199-224; Hilary Moore, *Burning Earth, Changing Europe: How the Racist Right Exploits the Climate Crisis and What We Can Do about It* (Brussels: Rosa Luxemburg Stiftung, 2020). Within the contemporary North American alt-right, as Blair Taylor notes, "some dispute climate change as a 'cultural Marxist' lie while others accept its reality but direct blame onto immigration, the third world, or 'globalism.'" Taylor, "Alt-right ecology: Ecofascism and far-right environmentalism in the United States" in Forchtner, ed., *The Far Right and the Environment*, 275-92, quote on 286.

45 Moore, *Burning Earth, Changing Europe*, 11. For a range of viewpoints compare James Morton Turner, "'The Specter of Environmentalism': Wilderness, Environmental Politics, and the Evolution of the New Right" *Journal of American History* 96 (2009), 123-48; John Hultgren, "The 'Nature' of American Immigration Restrictionism" *New Political Science* 36 (2014), 52-75; Efadul Huq and Henry Mochida, "The Rise of Environmental Fascism and the Securitization of Climate Change" *Projections* March 30, 2018; Alexander Ruser and Amanda Machin, "Nationalising the Climate: Is the European Far Right Turning Green?" *Green European Journal* September 27, 2019; James McCarthy, "Authoritarianism, Populism, and the Environment" *Annals of the American Association of Geographers* 109 (2019), 301-13.

46 Even Julius Evola, darling of today's alt-right, celebrated blood and soil during the fascist era. In *Erhebung wider die moderne*

Welt (Stuttgart: Deutsche Verlags-Anstalt, 1935), Evola invoked "Blut und Boden" (145) and extolled "the organic, living feeling for the soil" proper to land "that the Aryan race has conquered" (146). In 1941 Evola declared that once Fascism's heroic war destroyed the democracies, Italy would be able to re-embrace "the ideal of the feudal aristocracy, faithful to its own blood and its own soil," which would allow an "organic sense of nature" to flourish at last against Jewish "rationalism" and "materialism" (Evola, "Sulle origini remote della crisi italiana ed europea" *Dottrina Fascista* January 1941, 9-17, quotes on 11 and 14). Latter-day fans of Evola laud him as a forerunner to deep ecology: Giovanni Monastra and Philippe Baillet, *Piété pour le cosmos: Les précurseurs antimodernes de l'écologie profonde* (Saint-Genis-Laval: Éditions Akribeia, 2017).

47 Kyle Boggs, "The rhetorical landscapes of the 'alt right' and the patriot movements: Settler entitlement to native land" in Forchtner, ed., *The Far Right and the Environment*, 293-309, quote on 295. Much of the history of North American nature preservation is indeed directly based on stolen Native land; see Mark Spence, *Dispossessing the Wilderness: Indian Removal and the Making of the National Parks* (Oxford: Oxford University Press, 1999); Philip Burnham, *Indian Country, God's Country: Native Americans and the National Parks* (Washington: Island Press, 2000); Theodore Binnema and Melanie Niemi, "Wilderness, Conservation, and the Exclusion of Aboriginal People from Banff National Park in Canada" *Environmental History* 11 (2006), 724-50.

48 Taylor, "Alt-right ecology," 278. Taylor's essay is an excellent resource on the ecological politics of the alt-right. For additional context see Shane Burley, *Fascism Today: What It Is and How to End It* (Oakland: AK Press, 2017), 16, 111-12, 114-15, 127,

130, 137-38. Burley identifies biocentrism as "a key point on the environmental right, which has allowed crossover to movements like bioregionalism, Earth First!, and the animal liberation movement." (115)

49   All quotations from "The Alt-Right is Green" by "Evolalinkola," altright.com, July 26, 2017, part of a forum on "environmentalism and the alt-right" hosted at the site. The author's pseudonym is an amalgam of the names of Julius Evola and Pentti Linkola, the late deep ecologist who adopted unabashedly ecofascist positions. On the alt-right overlap with primitivist ideologies see Taylor, "Alt-right ecology," 284: "In recent years eco-fascist and alt-right groups have also embraced green, primitivist and anticivilization anarchist thinkers. These tendencies are united by a palingenetic impulse coupled with romantic longing for a prelapsarian universe of authenticity and ecological harmony unsullied by the corruption of modernity."

50   Jordan Dyett and Cassidy Thomas, "Overpopulation Discourse: Patriarchy, Racism, and the Specter of Ecofascism" *Perspectives on Global Development & Technology* 18 (2019), 205-24, quote on 206. Though popularized in environmental discourse in the 1970s, the rhetoric of "overpopulation" has a longer history, often bound up with eugenics. On the affiliation of ecological thinking with population anxieties in the UK and US from the 1920s to the 1950s see Robertson, *The Malthusian Moment*, 13-60; Powell, *Vanishing America*, 158-85; Björn Linnér, *The Return of Malthus: Environmentalism and Post-War Population-Resource Crisis* (Cambridge: Cambridge University Press, 2003), 36-40, 56-60, 102-16; Matthew Connelly, *Fatal Misconception: The Struggle to Control World Population* (Cambridge: Harvard University Press, 2008), 128-34; Alison Bashford, *Global Population: History, Geopolitics,*

and Life on Earth (New York: Columbia University Press, 2016), 157-80. The political background to these ideas is complex, but as Connelly observes, influential mid-century environmentalists were "obsessed with the undeserving poor" and held that "many poor people would not make it and must be left to die." (130) This is the tradition that gave rise to Hardin, Tanton, Foreman and the like.

51 George Hawley, *Right-Wing Critics of American Conservatism* (Lawrence: University Press of Kansas, 2016), 77. Hawley notes this tradition's "long association with racism" (80). See also the references to race and eugenics in Allan Carlson, *The New Agrarian Mind: The Movement Toward Decentralist Thought in Twentieth-Century America* (New Brunswick: Transaction, 2000).

52 Tom Brass, "The Agrarian Myth, the 'New' Populism and the 'New' Right" *Journal of Peasant Studies* 24 (1997), 201-45, quotes on 204.

53 Jack Healy, "Amid the Kale and Corn, Fears of White Supremacy at the Farmers' Market" *New York Times* August 19, 2019; the article appeared on the front page of the print edition of the newspaper. See also the analyses by Ellen Wu, "Bloomington 2019: 'The Year of the Farmers' Market Controversy'" *Limestone Post* December 30, 2019, and Michelle Niemann, "Organic Farming's Political History" *Edge Effects* January 23, 2020. As scholarship on the identitarian movement continues to develop, researchers have sometimes fallen back on wholly uncritical works like José Zúquete, *The Identitarians: The Movement against Globalism and Islam in Europe* (University of Notre Dame Press, 2018), which casts the far right as brave opponents of a "globalist oligarchy." For an antidote to such apologias under an "ethnographic" veneer see Agnieszka Pasieka, "Taking Far-Right Claims Seriously and Literally: Anthropology and the Study of Right-Wing Radicalism" *Slavic Review* 76 (2017), 19-29.

54 Alexandra Minna Stern, *Proud Boys and the White Ethnostate: How the Alt-Right Is Warping the American Imagination* (Boston: Beacon, 2019), 60; see 60-62 for her discussion of environmental themes in the contemporary North American far right.

55 Sarah Manavis, "Eco-fascism: The ideology marrying environmentalism and white supremacy thriving online" *New Statesman* September 21, 2018; Matthew Phelan, "The Menace of Eco-Fascism" *New York Review of Books* October 22, 2018; Tom Bennett, "Understanding the Alt-Right's Growing Fascination with 'Eco-Fascism'" *Vice News* April 10, 2019.

56 Quoted in Jeffrey Kaplan, ed., *Encyclopedia of White Power: A Sourcebook on the Radical Racist Right* (Walnut Creek: AltaMira Press, 2000), 226. For an insightful survey see Kevan Feshami, "A Mighty Forest Is Our Race: Race, Nature, and Environmentalism in White Nationalist Thought" *Drain Magazine* February 2020. Despite my reservations about the term, Feshami offers a perceptive diagnosis of the "white nationalism" concept.

57 "Aryan Destiny: Back to the Land" in Kaplan, ed., *Encyclopedia of White Power*, 488-91. In the 1990s Turner argued that "Aryan man should keep a vegetarian macrobiotic diet, preferably organically grown, and abstain from all processed and chemically produced food." (Gardell, *Gods of the Blood*, 189)

58 Michael Novick, *White Lies, White Power: The Fight Against White Supremacy and Reactionary Violence* (Common Courage Press, 1995), 205-08. According to Metzger's follower Wyatt Kaldenberg, "The reason the Aryan race is dying is because the Earth is dying." Kaldenberg, "Aryan Green Man Arise" (published in *White Aryan Resistance* in 1995), quoted in Gardell, *Gods of the Blood*, 179.

59 Katja Lane, ed., *The Revolutionary Writings of David Lane* (St. Maries: Fourteen Word Press, 1999), 97, 340. Lane was a seminal

figure in the violent racist underground of the US extreme right. See Kathleen Belew, *Bring the War Home: The White Power Movement and Paramilitary America* (Cambridge: Harvard University Press, 2018), 103-84.

60 Balša Lubarda, "Beyond Ecofascism? Far Right Ecologism as a Framework for Future Inquiries" *Environmental Values* 29 (forthcoming 2020) makes a sensible proposal for using the term "ecofascism" to refer to specifically fascist variants within the broader category of "far right ecologism." My own stance is similar, though in some contexts I use the term "fascist ecology" as the more specific designation and "right-wing ecology" as the general type, encompassing conservative, nationalist, and authoritarian strands in addition to the far right. For a more thorough examination see Peter Staudenmaier, "Right-wing Ecology in Germany: Assessing the Historical Legacy" in Janet Biehl and Peter Staudenmaier, *Ecofascism Revisited* (Porsgrunn: New Compass, 2011), 89-132.

61 While the El Paso massacre was aimed against primarily Latinx communities, the Christchurch shooter targeted mosques, reflecting a lethal combination of anti-Muslim and anti-immigrant prejudice. These crimes shine a harsh light on the ideological affinities between raging xenophobia and environmental motives. From the spate of media reports in the wake of the Christchurch and El Paso attacks see Peter Beinart, "White Nationalists Discover the Environment" *The Atlantic* August 5, 2019; Konstantin Nowotny, "Faschismus in grün?" *Freitag* August 5, 2019; Tess Owen, "Eco-Fascism: The Racist Theory That Inspired the El Paso and Christchurch Shooters" *Vice News* August 6, 2019; Dawn Stover, "White nationalism's solution to climate change: fewer brown people"

Bulletin of the Atomic Scientists August 6, 2019; Luke Darby, "What Is Eco-Fascism, the Ideology Behind Attacks in El Paso and Christchurch?" *GQ* August 7, 2019; John Eligon, "The El Paso Screed, and the Racist Doctrine Behind It" *New York Times* August 8, 2019; Graham Lawton, "White nationalists are perverting environmentalism to smear migrants" *New Scientist* August 14, 2019; Joel Achenbach, "Two mass murders a world apart share a common theme: 'Ecofascism'" *Washington Post* August 18, 2019; Joël Laforest, "In the fight against eco-fascism, we need to politicize nature" *Canadian Dimension* September 12, 2019; Damien Leloup, "Ecofascisme: Comment l'extrême droite en ligne s'est réappropriée les questions climatiques" *Le Monde* October 4, 2019; Cole Baker, "The Growing Threat of Ecofascism" *Geopolitical Monitor* January 16, 2020; Pinar Üzeltüzenci, "Humans are not the Virus: Why Ecofascism is Bad for You" *Mangal Media* April 29, 2020; Betsy Hartmann, "The Ecofascists" *Columbia Journalism Review* Spring 2020, 18-19.

62 All quotations from the Christchurch perpetrator's March 2019 manifesto, titled "The Great Replacement." Similar passages are strewn throughout the 87-page text, heralding "A path focusing on nature and respect for the environment" while decreeing that "the future of the White race" depends on "preserving and exulting nature and the natural order." For further discussion see the informed treatments by Bernhard Forchtner, "Eco-fascism: Justifications of terrorist violence in the Christchurch mosque shooting and the El Paso shooting" *Open Democracy* August 13, 2019; Sam Adler-Bell, "Why White Supremacists Are Hooked on Green Living: Eco-fascism is fashionable again on the far right" *New Republic* September 24, 2019; Beth Gardiner, "White Supremacy Goes Green" *New York Times* March 1, 2020; Jeff

Sparrow, *Fascists Among Us: Online Hate and the Christchurch Massacre* (London: Scribe, 2020), 81-93.

63 See the detailed argument by Tamara Mix, "The Greening of White Separatism: Use of Environmental Themes to Elaborate and Legitimize Extremist Discourse" *Nature & Culture* 4 (2009), 138-66. In a wider sense, the political flexibility of ecological tropes could be considered an instance of what Brian Drake has aptly called "nature's strange bedfellows" (Drake, *Loving Nature, Fearing the State: Environmentalism and Antigovernment Politics before Reagan*, University of Washington Press 2013, 3). The role of apocalyptic rhetoric in environmental contexts is a compelling example; see the fine analysis by Eddie Yuen, "The Environmental Movement and Catastrophism" in Sasha Lilley, ed., *Catastrophism: The Apocalyptic Politics of Collapse and Rebirth* (Oakland: PM Press, 2012), 15-43.

64 Compare Richard Smyth, "Nature writing's fascist roots" *New Statesman* April 5, 2019; Jessica Krzeminski, "Whose Utopia? American Ecofascism Since the 1880s" *Edge Effects* October 10, 2019; Bernhard Forchtner and Ana Tominc, "Balaclava Küche: Extreme Rechte—Veganismus—Lebensstil" in Hannah Dingeldein, ed., *Diskurse des Alimentären* (Münster: Lit, 2017), 209-26.

65 Moore, *Burning Earth, Changing Europe*, 9. Cf. Roderick Graham, "Inter-ideological mingling: White extremist ideology entering the mainstream on Twitter" *Sociological Spectrum* 36 (2016), 24-36; Mark Durie, "The eco-fascist ideology of the Christchurch killer" *Quadrant* 63 (2019), 14-18; Jarrod Gilbert and Ben Elley, "Shaved heads and sonnenrads: Comparing white supremacist skinheads and the alt-right in New Zealand" *New Zealand Journal of Social Sciences* 15 (2020), 280-94; Marc Tuters, "Esoteric Fascism Online: 4chan and the Kali Yuga" in Louie Valencia-

García, ed., *Far-Right Revisionism and the End of History* (New York: Routledge, 2020), 287-303.

66 Dorceta Taylor, "American Environmentalism: The Role of Race, Class and Gender in Shaping Activism 1820-1995" *Race, Gender & Class* 5 (1997), 16-62; Laura Pulido, *Environmentalism and Economic Justice: Two Chicano Struggles in the Southwest* (Tucson: University of Arizona Press, 1997); Ramachandra Guha, *The Unquiet Woods: Ecological Change and Peasant Resistance in the Himalaya* (Berkeley: University of California Press, 2000); Wangari Maathai, *The Green Belt Movement* (New York: Lantern, 2003); Mart Stewart, "Slavery and the Origins of African American Environmentalism" in Dianne Glave, ed., *To Love the Wind and the Rain: African Americans and Environmental History* (Pittsburgh: University of Pittsburgh Press, 2005), 9-20; Harvey Feit, "Myths of the Ecological Whitemen: Histories, Science, and Rights in North American – Native American Relations" in Michael Harkin, ed. *Native Americans and the Environment* (Lincoln: University of Nebraska Press, 2007), 52-92; Dianne Glave, *Rooted in the Earth: Reclaiming the African American Environmental Heritage* (Chicago Review Press, 2010); Connie Chiang, "Race and Ethnicity in Environmental History" in Andrew Isenberg, ed., *Oxford Handbook of Environmental History* (Oxford University Press, 2014), 573-99; John Claborn, *Civil Rights and the Environment in African-American Literature, 1895–1941* (London: Bloomsbury Academic, 2017); Dina Gilio-Whitaker, *As Long as Grass Grows: The Indigenous Fight for Environmental Justice from Colonization to Standing Rock* (Boston: Beacon, 2019); Julie Sze, *Environmental Justice in a Moment of Danger* (Oakland: University of California Press, 2020).

67 It is this combination that gives extreme right ecological politics

their volatile dynamism, counterposing an idealized nature to an irredeemably decadent society. As Chetan Bhatt remarks, "In contemporary fascism's dystopic imagination, primordial ecological unity has been mutilated by modern life." Bhatt, "White Extinction: Metaphysical Elements of Contemporary Western Fascism" *Theory, Culture & Society* (forthcoming 2020).

68 Adrian Parr, *Birth of a New Earth: The Radical Politics of Environmentalism* (New York: Columbia University Press, 2018), 67; see her chapter "Fascist Earth," 65-90, for fuller discussion.

69 Aristotle Kallis, "When Fascism Became Mainstream: The Challenge of Extremism in Times of Crisis" *Journal of Comparative Fascist Studies* 4 (2015), 1-24.